The End of Theology –
And the Task of Thinking about God

Also by George Pattison

Art, Modernity and Faith: Towards a Theology of Art
Kierkegaard: The Aesthetic and the Religious
Agnosis: Theology in the Void
Kierkegaard and the Crisis of Faith
Anxious Angels: A Retrospective View of Religious Existentialism
'Poor Paris!' Kierkegaard's Critique of the Spectacular City

With Stephen Platten

Spirit and Tradition: An Essay on Change

With Wendy Beckett

Pains of Glass

The End of Theology
– And the Task of
Thinking about God

George Pattison

SCM PRESS LTD

Copyright © George Pattison 1998

0 334 02753 5

First published 1998 by
SCM Press Ltd
9–17 St Albans Place London N I ONX

Typeset at The Spartan Press Ltd
Lymington, Hants
Printed in Great Britain by
Biddles Ltd, Guildford and King's Lynn

For Don Cupitt,
with gratitude for both stimulation and
provocation

Never will a work of man have a good issue if we do not think of the souls whom it is given us to help, and of the life between soul and soul, and of our life with them and of their lives with each other. We cannot help the coming of redemption if life does not redeem life

(Martin Buber)

Contents

    Language and its limits   122
    The literal and the figural   129
    From the verbal to the visual   135
    Towards the ethical   140

Acknowledgments

One of the central concepts of this book is the concept of dialogue, and dialogue has been an important element in the process of writing. Various parts of the present text have been read by or presented to a number of individuals and groups, and their comments have entered into the shaping of the final product. Amongst those whose interest and comments have been particularly encouraging (even when they haven't agreed with my particular line of argument) have been Don Cupitt, David Ford, Pippa Berry, Patrick Sheil, the students of the Lutheran University of Budapest and of the Peter Pazmany Catholic University of Hungary, members of the Modern Churchpeople's Union, the theology students of King's College and an inter-disciplinary group of graduate students, also of King's College. I am also grateful to John Bowden for his positive response to my original idea and his support in preparing the manuscript.

Introduction

Several features of this book call for some explanation. Most obviously (and despite the fact that it deals with a number of issues that are much written about in contemporary academic theology) it is a book without citations. Some readers may find this irritating, particularly if they are unable to identify the sources of the positions against which I am arguing. Nonetheless, this tactic is important to me because I do not want to get mired in the details of the individually variable ways of presenting the views against (or for) which I am taking up arms, nor, despite an occasionally polemical tone, do I wish to get involved in personalized polemics and confrontations. The resurgence of a polemical and adversarial tone in some recent theology is, I believe, fundamentally hostile to the pursuit of thinking about God. It seems to me that the issues are what they are, irrespective of their current representatives, and whilst it would be perfectly possible to name those I refer to as revelationists, or narrative theologians or radicals or whatever, to do so would commit me to writing a different kind of book.

Another unusual feature of the book is the use – some might think the excessive use – of the first person singular pronoun. This reflects a deep unease, and not a little impatience, both with regard to my own writing and that of others, with the ever-rising tide of secondariness in theological writing. Theology is a discipline with an extraordinarily long and tangled history, and it is consequently very easy for theologians to become commentators upon commentaries upon commentaries – and so on *ad infinitum*. That thinking about God requires engagement with the tradition and with its contemporary context is not something I wish to deny. However, it is all too easy for the contemporary theologian to defer the moment when it is necesary to stop and think, to ponder seriously the nature and direction of one's own thinking and to consider why one is committed to this particular way and what its consequences are. As we add our voice to the surging polyphony of the historical development of ideas, it is important that it really is our own voice. Thinking about God is not the business of technicians, but a matter of dialogue between embodied, living voices. If it is not, then we find ourselves in the situation at which we have, in fact, arrived – a situation marked by a constantly widening gap between the world of popular (and all too often populist) religious literature on the one hand and the hermetic universe of academic theology on the other. This, then, is an exercise in personal stock-taking. I do not know whether the views I advance here are true or whether they are even of interest to others, but I am committed to them. Adding a signature to work in the realm of ideas is something that many regard as problematic. I regard it as a necessary condition of our being able to begin.

It is also a necessary condition of our being able to sign off, to take leave and move on. It will be obvious from what follows that I do not wish to take leave of God. On the contrary, I would not dare say that I have yet arrived at a point at which I am really able to think the meaning of God with any great depth of insight. Precisely because the height, length, breadth and depth of God remain as yet unthought, there is occasion for the undertaking I call 'thinking about God'. But if I do not wish to take leave of God, I do wish to take leave of one particular way or complex of ways of attempting to think the reality called 'God', i.e., the way of theology as I have learned it and, somewhat confusedly, practised it. How much continuity there will turn out to be between where I have come from and where I now feel myself to be going cannot as yet be decided, and what conversations between myself and those who continue to serve the ancient banner of theology may still be to come remain clothed in the incognito of the future. Nonetheless, I hope the theologians do not take it as a gratuitous slap in the face. An argument centring on the principle of dialogue would be inconsistent if it sought to end rather than to stimulate conversation.

George Pattison,
King's College, Cambridge   25 May 1998

I

The End of Theology and the Task of Thinking about God

The crisis of theology

Western theology has reached a critical phase in its history. Assailed from without and subverted from within, the once proud Queen of the Sciences now finds herself having to eke out a living at the margins of academic life, foraging amongst the uncultivated borderlands of other disciplines.

This is the outcome of various events, ideas and pressures that have combined to form the culture and condition of modernity. Amongst these we might include the following: the theoretical critique of religious belief represented by thinkers like Hume, Kant, Feuerbach, Marx, Nietzsche, Freud and Simone de Beauvoir; the challenge posed by such horrific events as the battles of the First World War, the Nazi Holocaust, Hiroshima and Nagasaki; the impact of the scientific revolution and its associated technologies upon humanity's self-image, culminating in the radical challenge to humanism posed by contemporary genetic engineering; the internal critique of theological texts and foundations by radical theologians from D. F. Strauss via the theology-of-the-death-of-God of the 1960s through to Don Cupitt; globalization and the advent of religiously pluralistic societies. The result has been a centuries-long erosion of religious belief and theological authority in the Western world.

Today, when people seek to understand 'what the world is really like' they do not turn to the priest or to the theologian but to the scientist: the cosmologist who tells us how the world began, the evolutionary biologist who tells us how life developed, the psychologist who tells us (usually within a Darwinian framework) how the mind works, and perhaps even the social scientist, the economist, the historian or the moral philosopher who offer to tell us what makes us behave in certain ways and what the consequences of our behaviour might be. Some of those who represent these various sciences may be (and often are) themselves religious believers, but for the most part that belief can be reflected only obliquely, if at all, in their professional work. Academic practice, in the arts no less than in the sciences, is consistently secular. Even if the theologian is invited to the seminar, it is certainly not as a presiding chairperson, but as someone with a particular knowledge or expertise to be taken into account alongside that of others and evaluated in exactly the same terms as theirs. No longer Queen, but fellow-worker.

Now some might say this is an honourable enough role, if somewhat modest in comparison with former glories. In fact I shall argue for something of the kind, even though I have problems with the word 'theology' in relation to this new job-description, problems I shall come to in due course. However, this is almost certainly not how theology understood itself in the past, nor how many theologians still working understand their task.

For 'theology' seems to be chronically prone to the temptation to define itself in such a way as to make claims that seem to impact upon every field of human knowledge. More than most subjects, theology has a penchant for the big picture, for final truths and ultimate concerns. Even when, as is mostly now the case, theology refrains from interfering with the data and results of other sciences (as it did historically in debates about cosmology and evolution), it still reserves the right to decide on the final significance of scientific work and to prescribe the 'proper' scope of application of this work, theoretically or practically. That is not to say that the way in which it does this is imperialistic in any crude sense of the word. Much recent theology has shown a considerable willingness to listen. Nevertheless, there often remains an implication that in some sense 'theology' has the right to the last word. Science, sociology or psychology may set out the facts, but theology alone is equipped to evaluate them. Theology is not just a 'fellow-worker', but also a 'fellow-worker who understands'.

A number of years ago Anglo-Saxon theology became preoccupied with questions of the nature of religious language, often in connection with the philosophy of Ludwig Wittgenstein. It became fashionable to recast many of the classical questions of theology, questions about the nature and existence of God or the concept of prayer, so that they were no longer understood as being about how things are in the world, but as questions about how language is to be used. Such a move may at first glance seem to be in line with the repudiation of a metaphysical-overview understanding of theology. Yet, curiously (or not!), the old habits die hard, and even within this new paradigm of thinking, theologians became engrossed with the question of defining their own special and specific contribution. One phrase that had a certain currency at that time was that theologians were 'guardians of grammar'. This certainly sounds a lot more modest than many previous conceptions of the theologian's role, but on second glance it still perpetuated the view that theology has a certain privilege: i.e., that the theologian is qualified, in a way that no one else quite is, to adjudicate as to what is or isn't a fitting use of religious language. If this is qualified in such a way that the theologian's domain is limited to the church and is not extended to the academy or to society as a whole, then this is perhaps acceptable, as long as the structures of church life are themselves so ordered that the theologian really does speak for the church and not simply for a self-recruiting cadre within it.[1]

This is by no means to say that theologians are more than usually arrogant or hubristic individuals. On the contrary, I know many,

---

[1] The issue of the 'place' of theology is one I shall address in a later chapter.

and not a few are amongst the most self-effacing and modest of intellectuals. The issue is not one of personality but of conception: i.e., what it is we take the theologian to be, to do or to know; what it is that makes up 'his' (and, statistically at least – at the very least – the gender-specific pronoun is probably justified) specific and unique undertaking that makes him a theologian and not anything else.

The stone upon which all conceptions of theological privilege stumble is, from a certain point of view, stunningly obvious: *theology has no methodology of its own.* The skills required to be a working theologian are essentially skills shared by a range of workers in the humanities. They include philological, philosophical, historical and literary skills that may indeed occur in a unique combination in theology (although that too, in an age when the boundaries between, e.g., philosophy and literature are increasingly blurred, is increasingly difficult to maintain), but not in such a way as to give theology access to any data inaccessible to other sciences or to formulate arguments or conclusions unintelligible to other sciences. Naturally, by concentrating on a specific area of interest, the theologian will acquire a certain specialized knowledge that comes from reading texts, studying historical events or engaging with philosophical questions that are more or less neglected by others. Such specialization, however, only serves to differentiate theology from other disciplines in the humanities in the way that a historian of Byzantium is differentiated from a historian of ideas, or a student of Renaissance literature from a student of film studies. If it seems natural to turn first to the theologian for a view on the understanding of the eucharist amongst Anglican divines of the seventeenth century or information about the differences between Kierkegaard's christology and that of Karl Barth, such a move really says very little about the fundamental issue. A theologian is more likely than others to be interested in such matters, but they may also, for various reasons, very easily become the concern of students of literature, of historians, or of philosophers. The theologian may indeed come to possess a certain expertise, a certain style, a certain art, but that, I suggest, falls far short of what theology has generally believed to be necessary in order to do justice to its essential nature.

Let me be quite clear. This is not just a comment about how theology happens to be done in the departments of theology I am familiar with. It is, again, a question of the very conception of theology. Let me illustrate the point in the following way.

It is perfectly possible for a modern student of theology to gain the highest academic results, even if he or she doesn't believe in God. I have had students who exemplify this. 'Ah!' you might say, 'Such people are not, however, *really* theologians. Being a theologian is not just a question of passing exams; it demands an inner orientation of the spirit, a deep and passionate engagement with the things of God. Theology proper begins with penitence, continues in prayer and culminates in worship. We must apply to theology what has been said of the Christian artist: "To paint the things of Christ, it is first necessary to live with Christ." ' Fine, I accept this. Let us then say that there are theologians and – theologians. The one lot are 'merely' very bright students of religious studies, the others alone qualify as 'theologians' in the full sense of the word. Let us focus in on these latter. For them, it is undoubtedly true that the most important thing is their God-relationship, however that is conceived. At the end of the day they will submit to the view of Thomas Aquinas that in comparison with the vision of God itself, all human theological work is but chaff. In the meantime, however, they remain committed to that work, and seek to do it in such a way as to be true to the faith or the vision that moves them. But what about the work they produce, their 'theology', as it appears in lectures, papers, articles and books? If it is any good at all, it is going to have to answer to the normal standards of public discourse. It is going to have to articulate itself in such a way as to be understood by any well-meaning reader; its arguments are going to have to be rational, its use of evidence appropriate, its interpretations compelling, its visions imaginable, and so on. Whatever arcane meaning this theology may have for the theologian himself (or for the initiates who share this arcane 'knowledge') does not and cannot belong to its public face. Once it has come out into the open it has to promote, to argue and to defend its case by rules and with tools shared with those outside the fold. A knowing look, a tone of voice, a certain turn of phrase may signal a deeper wisdom, but if such deeper wisdom remains below the threshold of what can be publicly articulated, it is of no significance. If he is not to be convicted of special pleading or of belonging to the intellectual equivalent of a holy huddle, the theologian must take his place on the common ground of intellectual learning, teaching and research. A great many have gone a long way in this direction, but one still encounters a certain reserve around certain non-negotiable (or, as it is said, 'unsurpassable') affirmations. But is such a reserve acceptable in the context of an institution that is committed to complete freedom of research and expression? Surely it must be the case that in relation to God no less than to any other field of enquiry, there are no questions that cannot be asked and no positions that can be ruled out in advance.[2] Of course, no science, no human undertaking can pursue its goals without making certain assumptions or circumscribing the scope of the project concerned in such a way as to push certain questions and considerations into the background or unexamined penumbra of its operations. However, it is one thing to accept that one is always having to make presuppositions of this kind for pragmatic reasons, and quite another to make a virtue of necessity by declaring them to be out of reach of all further investigation – and it is something else again to say that there is an asymmetry between one's own discipline and all others such that one's own discipline (theology – but similar claims are sometimes made for philosophy) has a right to issue declarations about the foundations

---

[2] I shall revisit the question of the institutional 'place' of theology and thinking about God in more detail in Chapter 4 below.

and boundaries of other disciplines whilst refusing a reciprocal right of access.

Although I have been pursuing this question largely in terms of theology's relation to knowledge, as that is institutionalized in contemporary academic life, I indicated previously that it is not only intellectual pressures that have brought about the dethroning of theology. There have been moral and religious pressures as well. The event of the Holocaust, for example, is an event in the moral and religious order of a magnitude comparable to the Copernican or Darwinian revolutions in science, and its long-term impact on theology will, I suspect, be no less great than those tremendous transformative revolutions. Why is this? Certainly not because the human race was ignorant of its own capacity for evil prior to the years 1942–45. Massacres and cases of unspeakable institutiona-lized or individual cruelty are well-documented in almost every age of human history and almost every region of the inhabited earth. Nor was the unleashing of genocidal violence against Jews unprecedented. In the case of the Holocaust, however, we are dealing with an event that involved an almost unprecedented level of organization and planning, carried out over a considerable period of time and implicating most major European nationalities in varying degrees. It was also an event that was meticulously documented, with an abundance of bureaucratic records, photo-graphs, films, diaries, letters and memoirs, and this documentation makes it an issue for us, an awful, unavoidable, ugly fact that belongs to our history whether we like it or not. In considering the uniqueness of the Holocaust, or the way in which it marks a critical threshold for theology, it is perhaps also relevant to bear in mind its historical context: that this was not an event that took place in a remote, barbaric or primitive environment; this happened amongst peoples who were heir to centuries of Christian teaching and the beneficiaries of the intellectual, moral and scientific Enlightenment, as well as of a cultural history that produced some of the world's very greatest music, literature, philosophy and art. It is also an event that is not only staggering in its scale but also (perhaps precisely because of the way in which it has been documented) breaks down into individual stories, scenes and images that offer horrifying and absolutely singular insights into the possibilities of human degradation. After all, remembering Dostoevsky's Ivan Karamazov, we have to say that we don't need to accumulate thousands or millions of instances of suffering in order to begin to doubt whether God can be simultaneously all-powerful and all-good. It only takes one child's inconsolable misery to lay the axe to the root of the theological tree – and the Holocaust presents us with just such devastating stories of individual suffering.

The theoretical problem of theodicy, i.e. of how God can be 'justified' in the face of suffering, is not new, but the Holocaust raises it to a new pitch, to breaking-point and, perhaps, beyond. Here logic, language and explanation snap. Nothing we can say seems worth saying, although no event stands in greater need of explanation and understanding. Least of all can we long bear with any theological explanation that tries to accommodate this event within some larger divine plan, story or metaphysically consoling world-view. We dread being caught playing the role of Job's bogus comforters, offering platitudinous words of comfort that entirely miss the point.

And there is a particular problem for Christian theology, precisely because what made these victims the scapegoats of their society was their membership of a people defined from within and without over many centuries by its exclusion from the Christian world. This uncomfortable situation robs Christian theology of some of its most valued resources in responding to the challenge of theodicy. For many modern theologians have in fact shown themselves willing to try to modify traditional claims about God's all-powerfulness so as to be able to speak convincingly to those traumatized by the mass horrors of the modern era. One element in this strategy is a refocussing of the theological vision away from God the Almighty Father seated on his heavenly throne, to Jesus, the suffering Saviour, nailed in emptiness and weakness to the cross of the world's agony. Only in Christ, only in the Crucified God, it has been said, can we find an appropriate set of symbols in which to begin to address questions of evil and suffering.[3] To the Jewish victims of the Holocaust, however, such claims, however well-intended, must seem like the deepest insult. If their fate is to be made intelligible by equating their suffering in Auschwitz with the suffering of Christ on the cross, then that must seem like just one more act of Christian imperialism, one more sorry chapter in the long history of denying Judaism its own identity, its own destiny, its own truth.[4] In terms of the problematic status of theology it once more betrays the theologian's inability to keep silent, his constitutional determination to be a man for all seasons. But, naturally, for the theologian to stay silent here is, in effect, to say that theology is not able to understand the riddle of God's dealings with the world and that precisely at the point where the need of an answer is most keenly felt, theology has nothing to say.[5]

The point we have come to is this: that in relation to the tasks of getting to know what the world is really like and who we ourselves really are (where we have come from, where we going and what we are capable of), the theologian *has nothing special to say*.

Back to, and beyond, 'Being'

As I write these words, I wonder how you, the reader, will respond to them. I do not like to shock, and yet I am afraid that some will be shocked. I do not like to provoke anger or hurt, but some may

---

[3] Even before the Holocaust some theologians were already saying such things, especially in response to the horrors of the First World War.

[4] This is not to say that the cross is irrelevant to Auschwitz. Clearly, many of those who died in the camps were Christians who found their last hope in the cross. Nor can we deny the possibility that some Jews themselves may spontaneously reappropriate the cross as a symbolic focus for their self-understanding in response to the Holocaust. Where the problems begin is the point at which it is claimed that the cross is an exclusive means of comprehending this incomprehensible horror.

[5] Yet, paradoxically, theology is perhaps at its best when, in this case, it joins the rest of humanity in a stunned and uncomprehending silence.

feel angry or hurt. I suspect, however, that many will regard what I am saying as so obvious and so self-evident as scarcely to be worth saying at all. If that is so, or if even a significant minority of readers react in that way, it goes to show how rapidly things have changed.

Think back to what remains the most notorious work of radical theology written in England this century, John Robinson's *Honest to God*. Robinson provoked a massive controversy by suggesting that we should relinquish the God of theism, a personal being, inhabiting some sort of cosmic space outside the universe known to science. Instead, Robinson suggested, we should re-envisage 'Him' in terms of 'the Ground of Being', an expression Robinson took (with due acknowledgment) from another radical theologian, Paul Tillich. The idea of God as Ground of Being was, in Robinson's view, far less encumbered with historical, scientific, philosophical or psychological baggage than the traditional God, creating the world and interfering in its running whenever things got a bit out of hand (in a manner somewhat reminiscent of Britain's way of running its Empire). The 'Ground of Being' suggested a divinity within the world, yet in some important way deeper, more primordial, more fundamental than any particular being or group of beings within the world. Consequently, for theology to make the 'Ground of Being' the explicit object of its intellectual quest would be to endow its theological concerns with an ultimacy that no other discipline could ever hope to match. A theology shaped by its pursuit of 'the Ground of Being' might not want to claim any Queenly throne, but it might still want to claim a certain priority over other disciplines in terms of 'depth'. Robinson may have tried to redraw the cosmic hierarchy assumed by most previous theologizing, but it is not clear whether he really confronted the intellectual hierarchizing that seems to be characteristic of the theologian.

There were some (but not many) who judged *Honest to God* to have pulled its punches. But for most the question was: has this gone too far? And if one goes as far as this, what is there left for theology to think or say? Isn't this merely secularism in another guise?

However, from the point of view with which I have approached the question here, we can see that Robinson was very much in the mainstream of theology's thinking about itself. For the characteristic gesture of theology is not that it avails itself of the tools of Platonism or Aristotelianism or Historical Method or Existentialism, but that it postulates an all-encompassing and unsurpassable overview of the whole field of human knowledge and behaviour.

If, thirty-five years ago, that postulate was itself scarcely controversial, and was largely shared by theologians on both sides of the *Honest to God* debate, the intellectual landscape has now changed almost beyond recognition. Postmodernism in its myriad forms has swept the humanities, and we have arrived at a situation where anyone who claims any kind of unitary or synthetic vision is likely to prove the object of universal ridicule, and Robinson's 'Ground of Being' is immediately recognized as belonging to the metaphysics that 'we' (i.e. we postmodernists) have 'overcome' (or want to overcome or are in the process of overcoming).

Now, any reader of publishers' catalogues knows that some theologians have responded to this situation by becoming postmodern themselves. Here it is, of course, difficult to generalize, although it looks likely that a number of essentially incompatible movements are availing themselves of the *lingua franca* of contemporary academic exchange and, under the umbrella of postmodernism, sounding more similar than they really are. We must test the spirits! Thus there are those postmodern 'theologies' that have probably stopped being theologies at all in any traditional sense. On the other hand there are also some 'postmodern' theologies that are essentially a new conservatism, availing themselves of postmodernism's assault on the modernist critics of religion to reclaim their ancient privileges (although, naturally, in a 'post-metaphysical' way).

In order to see just what is going on here, let us go back, briefly, to Robinson's 'Ground of Being'. Amongst other things, that term plays on one of the oldest words in the theologian's manual, 'Being'.

'Being', in its special philosophical sense, is not a biblical word, and theology owes it to that other great source of European thought: Greek philosophy. That does not, however, mean that theology took the term over without adaptation, nor that there was a simple and agreed meaning attached to 'Being' in Greek philosophy itself. If, in the manner of a thumbnail sketch, we say that 'Being' was regarded by the Greeks as the highest and most universal metaphysical concept – that which is itself the being of everything that is – , we would immediately have to qualify this in a number of ways. We might, for example, note that Plato speaks of the Good as in some mysterious way prior to or 'beyond' Being. Again, we might observe how, in Aristotle, 'Being' is sometimes assimilated to 'Essence' or 'Substance', that is, that which makes a thing the sort of thing it is. Thus, the 'being' of a tree would consist in that which makes a tree a tree and not a flower or a shrub, whilst the 'being' of the vegetable kingdom would be that which makes vegetables vegetables and not animals or minerals. We can of course immediately see here the prospect of a hierarchization of Being, with more or less universal kinds of Being presenting themselves to view. Although the specific being of a tree is not shared by all plant life, the tree shares in the more general being that belongs to plant life as such, and that in turn shares in the still more general being that belongs to all living things, and they in turn share in the being that belongs to all existent things – Being with a capital 'B'. However, when we reach this point, it is hard to say exactly what this most universal kind of being is, or how it could be the object of a special science in the way that, say, animals or plant life are the objects of special sciences such as zoology or botany. The more general the concept is, the more vacuous and indefinable it seems. On the other hand, the metaphysical cast of mind requires some such highest concept or principle in order to ensure the unity of all those entities, the things that are or that exist and that constitute the field of all possible knowledge and action.

If this is unclear (and some philosophers would say that all such metaphysical talk is indeed intrinsically incoherent), this much can be said: that although the principle of Being is conceived metaphysically as the highest Being, the keystone (or, to mix metaphors, the foundation) that holds the whole realm of beings together, it does not need to be thought of as either personal or transcendent. It guarantees the knowability and coherence of the world but is not obviously supernatural, and it gives order to the realm of beings by inhering within it, not by having 'created' it from nothing. Moreover, we can ascend to the knowledge of this Being by means of reason, by reflecting on experience and on the conditions of experience, and, some would say, by means of a direct and infallible intuition, a vision of Being-Itself.

Yet even if Being in this absolute, metaphysical sense is not identical with the God of the Judaeo-Christian tradition, Being and God do seem to share certain important functions, and it was very easy for those who sought to synthesize the classical and biblical inheritance of early Christianity to identify Being with God, without being aware of any profound difficulties in so doing. Moreover, they soon found a text on which to hang their project: Exodus 3.14. This verse belongs to the story of Moses' encounter with God at the Burning Bush on Mount Horeb, when, having been commanded to return to Egypt in order to set the Israelites free from slavery, Moses asks God to tell him His name, so that he can tell the Israelites who it is who has sent him. 'God said to Moses, "I AM WHO I AM. This is what you are to say to the Israelites: I AM has sent me to you."'

In his epochal fusion of Christianity and Platonism, St Augustine appealed on many occasions to this verse as providing biblical evidence for the view that the Being of the philosophers and the God of the Christians was one and the same, with the qualification that the Christians knew Him in a different and superior manner, because they knew Him through His personal Incarnation in Jesus Christ. The view of the philosophers was a view from afar: true as far as it went but unable to give saving knowledge (an important point in a culture in which – unlike their modern counterparts –

philosophers claimed to offer precisely that). The same identification continued to be made throughout the centuries, reinforced by Thomas Aquinas in his synthesis of Christianity and Aristotelianism. For Aquinas, God is the Being – the one and only being – whose very Being is simply *to be*. If the being of a tree is to be a plant, with roots and branches (etc.), God's Being is nothing other than *to be*. In this way He completely actualizes Himself, i.e. he completely IS Himself without remainder, in the entirety of His existence.

It is easy for us to accuse these Christian philosopher-theologians of reading into the biblical text views they had acquired from philosophical sources, and contemporary biblical criticism has made quite different readings available. The charge has also been made that in doing so they vulgarized the philosophical content of the concept of Being itself. Yet the move they made was perhaps necessary and belonged to the inner orientation of theology. Obviously the Bible did not speak the same language as Greek philosophy and, in many ways, had a quite different set of concerns. Nonetheless, even if the text as it stands contains a residue of earlier, more primitive, more localized conceptions of God (such that 'God' in some passages seems to be little more than the local deity of a mountain or region and is merely one god – even if the strongest – amongst many), the full picture of God that emerges from the Bible is that God, like the Being of the philosophers, is the ground and guarantor of the existence and being of all that is: His thought, His resolve and His action are alone able to cause beings to come into existence or to be cut off from it. It is God who makes reality really real – and different as their methods and interests were, the Hebrew writers and the Greek philosophers were alike engaged by this most fundamental question: What, in this world of change and chance, can count as really real? What abides when everything else succumbs to time and tide? What is able to be without depending on anything or anyone else, simply by virtue of its own inner power?

The word 'ontology', the study of or discourse about Being, is, of course, a word derived from the Greek language. It is not a biblical word. However, in the light of my preceding remarks, can we not say that the biblical writers were, in their own way, developing – or, at the very least, assuming – a certain ontology, a certain way of describing and determining what makes beings be, a certain way of deciding what counts as really real?

Some theologians – perhaps most Protestant theologians – in the twentieth century have sought to maximize the *differences* between philosophy and theology. Philosophy is a work of human reason, starting from humanity and allowing its agenda to be determined by humanity's desires, needs and capacity for knowledge. Any knowledge of God attainable by philosophy cannot amount to more than a projection of humanity's own self-image. For theologians of this school, Feuerbach's charge that 'the secret of theology is anthropology' is legitimate when directed against liberal or humanistic expressions of faith. Theology proper, it is said, proceeds quite differently. On the principle that 'through God alone can God be known', true theology, *Christian* theology, begins with God's self-revelation attested by scripture, cutting across the presumed knowledge of God derived from other sources (i.e., philosophy), that is in fact not knowledge of God but just an inverted form of humanity's self-knowledge. Ontology, understood as a part, perhaps the fundamental part, of philosophy, is thus of no concern to theologians.

In many respects this repudiation of ontology carries forward a centuries-old aversion to philosophizing on the part of theologians who stand in the tradition of Luther and Calvin, a tradition epitomized in Luther's references to 'the whore Reason'. On the other hand, it enables some theologians to argue for a convergence between Christian theology and postmodern philosophy that strikes a chord quite different in tone from that of classical Protestantism. The argument hinges on the view that postmodern philosophy has itself moved 'beyond' ontology in an obscure yet epochal way. The doctrine of Being that provided the unifying thread of the story of philosophy from, say, Plato to, say, the early Heidegger has (it is said) been shown to depend upon a historically limited and historically relative set of assumptions. Now the limitations and relativity of these assumptions have been exposed, we are no longer bound by them and can set about a new kind of philosophizing. This will be a philosophy devoid of hierarchies, in which no special privilege is accorded to the objective kind of knowledge favoured by rationalistic 'male' reason.

The rhetoric of such post-metaphysical theology, speaking from 'beyond Being', is appealing and bears a superficial resemblance to what I am proposing here. The difference, however, is instructive, since, in my view, it is not possible to abandon ontology and still go on talking about 'theology' in any meaningful sense. The point has already been made that 'ontology' is not a biblical word, and yet (to repeat, in stronger terms, what I have already said) theology is, as such, inherently and massively ontological in its commitments. Abandon these, and whatever you are left with is no longer theology (a point many conservative critics of liberal, modernist and postmodernist theology are only too happy to make).

What, then, of the claim of revelationism, the claim that the biblical testimony is a full, perfect and sufficient resource that is the exclusive basis for any knowledge of God? And what of the associated claim that this differentiates theology from all philosophical ontology?

The short answer is that the claim simply cannot stand, unless one is prepared to regard the Bible in its entirety as devoid of significant references to matters of history and of fact. As well as the revelationists, some narrative theologians seem to want to move in this direction. They draw attention to the way in which the biblical text is shaped as story, moulded by metaphor, and embedded in worship and discipleship. Let us immediately concede that the Bible is of course not simply a collection of proof texts illustrating metaphysical truths, nor yet a queer sort of history book. However, such theologians would also be likely to reject the programme of demythologizing put forward in the 1940s, a programme that flows from the judgment that the biblical text is an expression in the language and mythology of its time of the existential commitments of its authors and, in so far as it is addressed to us, a call upon our commitment, without regard to the world view that we ourselves inhabit. In other words, they would reject the view that the language of the Bible is radically translatable into the language of the contemporary world without remainder. On the contrary, they insist, the language, stories and images of the Bible are unsurpassable and inexchangeable, and can consequently only be understood from within. *Inter-* (or even *intra*)textuality is the key, and, unless we are prepared to absorb ourselves in the biblical (and, some would add, the ecclesial) story in the terms offered by the text itself, we will never arrive at a significant understanding of its message. The medium, indeed, *is* the message.

Now such a view may refrain, or appear to refrain, from ontological claims, and to operate in an ethereal medium compounded of text, liturgy, prayer and practice, without regard either to questions concerning the metaphysical constitution of the world or to what is actually the case within the world. Unfortunately, this abstention removes the basis for any claim that the language of belief and/or theology is uniquely privileged. It becomes impossible to argue whether Christianity or Buddhism or humanism provides a better or more adequate frame of reference for probing the demanding ethical questions of the day, since all such 'stories' are regarded as incommensurable: one can only narrate how, within the framework of one particular story, one arrives at this particular set of moral imperatives.

Something very odd is going on here. On the one hand, theology is privileged in terms as unquestioning as those implied by the revelationists' adage 'through God alone can God be known'. Thus far, narrative theology stands in the line of revelationism and seems to share the revelationists' aim of immunizing theology to criticism from without.[6] On the other hand, there is a rather complacent

---

[6] Nor should we allow the charge to be confused by the fact that some of these theologians (though not all) are politically on the left. 'The left', as the twentieth century taught us only too clearly, is well able to breed its own brands of authoritarianism and illiberalism.

acceptance of the relativism of language-games, moral frameworks, and legitimating stories. Is this a neo-conservatism that has substituted a policy of withdrawal for one of confrontation, making a tactical retreat behind the monastery wall of religious introversion (a theological equivalent, perhaps, to what psychologists call the attitude of passive aggression), or is it a postmodern relativism that dare not speak its name?

To the extent that the uniqueness and untranslatability of the Christian story is emphasized, I am inclined to believe the former, but then, if that is correct, such theologies are going to have to face a series of simple yet devastating questions that they character-istically avoid, questions like these: What is it that is going to make someone who is not already living 'within' this story choose to do so? Wherein does its superiority lie? Why is it to be preferred above all others? If the theologian with whom I am arguing responds by saying that he is not interested in whether anybody else joins his band of story-tellers and that it is not especially privileged, but just happens to be the story he's involved in, then that's fine – but I shall have to conclude that he is, after all, a relativist, and that his story is indeed as devoid of ontological claims as the live role-playing games enjoyed by many modern teenagers (and some bank managers). The moment he wants to tell me that it's something more than that, however, then I am being asked to believe that his story is in some way a statement of or a response to the way things really are in the world, or the way human beings really are, and, because of the unique importance that he attaches to this story in shaping his life choices, I am in fact being asked to believe that *this* story (and no other) provides access to the really real. It is not just more real than live role-playing; it is that story than which no realler story can be told. I must draw a similar conclusion if the conversation takes an academic turn and my theological interlocu-tor, no matter how cautiously, takes it upon himself to circumscribe the scope or field of any non-theological discipline and to decree what can or cannot be known within that discipline. For that is to use the protection of theological privilege to predetermine not only what is knowable, but also what is really real. We are, it seems, back with ontology – and let us not be deceived by the fact that we have managed to shed the language of classical philosophy, for it is not the form of words that matters, but the claims being made.

Indeed, it is hard to see how it could be otherwise, if God remains an essential part of the story. For what is God, if not the criterion and source of the really real? If anyone wants to describe God as 'love', 'joy', 'blessedness', 'Father', or whatever, but also maintains that these descriptions have no purchase upon Being (however that is understood), i.e., that they are not ontological, how can we really consider such a person to be still a *theo*logian? If God has been required to renounce all claims to influence reality, can He still 'be' God?

We are, curiously, back with Robinson and his honesty before God, because the one thing that Robinson was sure he could not give up on was that God was the 'Ground of Being' – what I am calling 'the really real'. This confidence did, I believe, genuinely reflect the mainstream of theology's self-understanding – but it is only unquestionable as long as we remain within the perspective of theology itself.

The failure of ontology

But can the claim that theology has to do with the Ground of Being, the really real, be justified to non-theologians? Indeed, can the project of ontology be carried through at all by any single science or method of understanding? My contention is that it cannot. I shall try to explain why.

Over the millennia, many philosophers and theologians have attempted to provide arguments for the existence of God, under-stood in the sense of Being Itself or the Supreme Being. Generally speaking, these arguments are now widely assumed to fail, although some regard them as having a certain value in clarifying what is meant by 'God', even if they fall far short of proof in the full sense of the word. The need for a first cause to get the world rolling and the fear of an infinite regress in explanation; the radical instability of created being and the accompanying thought that, unless the existence of some absolute Being is assumed, the world would long ago have fallen into nothingness; the perfection of design visible in nature – these are some of the key elements in these proofs, familiar to every first-year theology student. However, since the rise of empirical science such ways of arguing have come to seem less and less persuasive. In the way they establish their claims about the existence and characteristics of an unobservable Being, they defy what science regards as the basic principles of provability. They cannot add to our knowledge of how things really are. According to Kant all arguments based on considerations concerning the world boil down to one single argument or, rather, conviction: that the world must really be as we conceive it to be. Kant did not, of course, mean by this that anything I happen to think about the world must be true. What he meant was that the laws of thought require me to think of the world as a unity, governed by law and consistent with itself. Science, in setting out to make a picture of the world, would never get anywhere if it regarded the world as utterly random and chaotic in such a way that anything could happen at any time without any statistical predictability. Science has to assume in advance the intelligibility of its object if it is to make any progress at all.

So where does God come in? God, according to Kant, is that concept which alone underwrites such a view of things. In affirming the existence of God, considered as the Supreme Being, the Really Real, I am affirming the intelligibility and coherence of the world. The best picture of the world I can come up with is of a regular, law-bound whole or system, whose secrets are susceptible to the methods of scientific investigation. The problem is, however, that I can never know whether it really is like that. I can never get behind my assumption of God's existence but, equally, I can never prove it either. Strangely, then, Kant had to affirm the necessity of the concept of God, the Really Real, but remained agnostic as to God's reality. Ontology was necessary, but problematic.

Now, obviously, Kant is only one name in the history of philosophy, and we cannot simply take Kant's word for this or any other philosophical statement. Religious thinkers in particular have been impatient with the kind of ontological scepticism Kant seems to have required of them. The kind of revelationism discussed earlier in this chapter was, in part, one such theological reaction. Kantian scepticism, it was claimed, is precisely the best that any merely human philosophy is going to be able to come up with. Revelation, however, *can* guarantee what science can only postulate problematically (and historically it is no accident that the early theology of Karl Barth, one of the strongest and most compelling expressions of such a view, developed in a context dominated by Neo-Kantianism). The problem is that this 'guarantee' is self-referential and self-policing: in the last resort revelationism has no evidence for its claims other than the claim that they are true or compelling. Its logic is that of the children's hymn allegedly cited by Karl Barth when asked for a one-sentence summary of his theology: 'Jesus loves me, this I know, for the Bible tells me so.' Fine, but why should I believe the Bible? If I am told it is self-authenticating, then that is also fine, but what if it doesn't authenticate itself to me or to the neighbour for whose salvation I am compassionately concerned? The question is all the sharper when put to a consistent revelationist who will not allow me to argue for the veracity of the Bible either on the basis of historical investigation or by appealing to the value of the Bible's moral teaching or its value as a profoundly and beautifully poetic expression of the human spirit, since all of these lines of defence in fact subordinate the Bible to non-biblical criteria. If I defend the Bible in this way, I am actually admitting that what really matters to me is historical fact, moral teaching or aesthetic sensibility. Ultimately, therefore, revelationism turns out to be an appeal to authority, but this 'authority' has no force other than the appeal itself. It is not really an exercise in logic or metaphysics at all, but a piece of powerful and compelling rhetoric. A rhetorical *tour de force* (and Barthian theology is indeed that) cannot, however, be treated as constitutive of anything that would count as knowledge.

But there have been other ways of attempting to break the spell of the Kantian taboo and to relaunch the project of ontology. One that has become increasingly influential in the wider cultural situation as well as in the church (though perhaps less amongst academic theologians) has been the way of mysticism.

This has taken many forms, from the more or less emotional to the more or less intellectual, from the ecstatic and the visionary to the silent and contentless. Some mystics have claimed to be carried beyond the world into the realm of the transcendent, whilst others have spoken only of insight into the unifying power at the heart of the world itself. And if the more popular images and concepts of mysticism have been shaped more by Hindu and Buddhist traditions than by Christianity, Christianity (like Judaism and Islam) has its own mystical traditions as well as its contemporary practitioners.

It is obviously dangerous to generalize about such a rich and culturally varied phenomenon, if, indeed, it can be said to constitute a single phenomenon at all. Within the limits of my present concern, however, the important claim arising out of the mystical literature, popular and academic, is that we can have a direct, immediate and incorrigible experience or intuition of the Really Real. Mystics accept the failure of reason and of revelation in the face of the mystery of Being with equanimity, because they believe themselves to have another – and infinitely quicker – route to the same goal.

Let us grant the mystics their claim to such a face-to-face encounter with the Really Real and accept their sense of divine immediacy in its own terms. The problem is, then what?

The mystics' embarrassment is neatly summed up in Wittgenstein's famous formula: 'Whereof we cannot speak, thereof we must keep silent' – or, as a Buddhist proverb has it: 'Those who know, do not say; those who say, do not know.' As the mystics' own writings repeatedly emphasize, and as commentators such as William James have long recognized, ineffability, indescribability and a beyond-wordsness seem to be vital elements of the mystical. Whatever the nature of the mystics' experience or intuition may be in itself, the moment it is expressed verbally (or, for that matter, in significant gesture, visual form or music) it enters into a world of signs and symbols that is essentially public. At this point the mystics have to make a quick decision. Either their experience *can* be expressed in language, or it cannot. If it can, then it is hard to see what the experience can add to the force of any doctrinal statement or symbol, since it has been conceded that the statement or symbol is intelligible to others who have not themselves had the experience. Its meaning is justifiable in the same terms and by the same means as any other linguistically or symbolically encoded meaning. If it cannot, then it places itself by definition outside the domain of theology, understood as a way of knowing directed towards explicating the nature of reality.

Let us take an example. The mystic (or the mystic's apologist) claims to have had a direct intuition in a divine darkness of unknowing of the essence of divine Being, an immediate apprehension of Being Itself in its super-rational, super-cognitive actuality. Can this claim be taken as 'evidence' for the theological argument that God is Being Itself, the Being whose essence it is To Be?

It is hard to see how that could be the case. Apart from the difficulty that mystics describe their experiences in diverse terms, there is a fundamental incommensurability between the experience and its use as evidence in theological argument. Even if all the mystics there had ever been were united in saying that their vision, although 'beyond words', was a vision of God as Being Itself and, as such, confirmed theological statements to the same effect, I would still have a problem. Again, this would boil down to an either/or. Assuming that I have not had such an experience myself, my assent to the mystics' claims would either be on the basis of understanding those claims or it would not. If it did involve understanding them, then it is clear that the claims do not require the testimony of experience to justify their intelligibility and force. In this case, I probably believe God to be Being Itself, because (for example) my Aristotelian reason tells me so (not to mention Exodus 3.14 or the fact that the church might have authoritatively declared the mystic concerned to be a saint and 'doctor of the church', like Teresa of Avila). The person who steps forward and declares 'And I have experienced it to be so!' does not clinch my conviction but merely corroborates it and, probably, I'm pleased to have them on board. But even if I don't accept the possibility of such an experience this side of the Last Judgment (and many Christian Aristotelians, medieval and modern, don't), that is not going to prevent me from holding on to my fundamental conception of God as Being Itself. That conception stands or falls in its own terms. If, on the other hand, I do not understand the mystics' claim, but assent to it all the same, then mysticism is playing the same role that the Bible plays for the revelationist and is open to the same objection: that it constitutes an authoritarian gesture – 'Believe what I say, because I say it.'[7]

Mysticism, then, seems not to provide a good basis for ontology. Even if the mystics experience Being Itself or the Really Real, they cannot tell us anything about it that we do not already know, and if we have other reasons for believing that we have in fact no significant knowledge of Being, then the mystics will be unable to persuade us otherwise – unless or until we come to share their experience.

If revelationism (together with its postmodern descendant, narrative theology) and mysticism fail to break the post-Kantian blockade of ontology, what other options remain?

We could, of course, leave theology for a moment and consider whether there are any purely philosophical attempts to restart

---

[7] Assuming, that is, that we are dealing with a mystic who wants to use mystical experience as legitimation for holding or privileging certain theological propositions or symbols. There are, of course, mystics whose testimony is of a more oblique or indirect kind, who cannot simply be equated with the 'theological' mystics. Such quietistic souls are content that their testimony should have no greater status than poetry, myth or symbol.

ontological thinking and, if so, whether they offer any prospects of success.

One option would be that pursued by the philosophical movement known as phenomenology, particularly in the version developed by Martin Heidegger.

Heidegger's early masterpiece, *Being and Time* (1927), opens by raising the question of Being and asks, in a radical way, whether we are still able even to ask the question. We, the children of the secular age, are, it seems, metaphysically dispossessed, immersed in the world of immediate, short-term and local undertakings and understandings, without any vision of the whole. In this situation, Heidegger asks, is it at all possible to re-open the question of Being? Can we even understand what it would mean to ask such a question, let alone be able to understand any 'answer' that might be given to it?

In posing these questions, Heidegger insists that he himself has no advantage over his readers, no privileged knowledge, no mystical experience denied to others. All he has to go on is the world of everyday life, and the way in which we generally understand that world.

Thus far at least Heidegger follows his teacher Husserl, the founder of the phenomenological movement, who insisted that the phenomenologist had to restrict himself to the world of phenomena, the world of appearances (i.e., *how things seem to us*), while 'bracketing off' any consideration as to whether these appearances are 'real' or 'true' in any ontological sense. Heidegger, however, wants to be able both to start with the world of everyday phenomena *and* to get a grip on the question of Being. Can it be done?

One important element in *Being and Time* that is sometimes overlooked by commentators (and that was certainly often overlooked by Heidegger's contemporaries) is that Heidegger is not primarily observing people's social behaviour or psychological attitudes. All he relies on, he says, is how, for the most part, we talk about ourselves, because it is in the way in which we talk about ourselves that we disclose our assumptions as to the meaning that life has for us. Obviously this involves Heidegger in making a judgment as to which of the many discourses current in the modern world is most characteristic. The one he hits upon is, loosely speaking, existentialistic, Christian in origin but secular in outlook, and represented (in the 1920s) by writers like Kierkegaard, Dostoevsky, Kafka, Spengler, Hesse and, indeed, Karl Barth. If we attend to what 'modern man' says about himself, Heidegger argues, we will learn that he is absorbed in day-to-day tasks, communicates by means of second-hand knowledge and passes on ideas and beliefs without penetrating their inner meaning. Happily or unhappily, he is one of the crowd, the anonymous 'they', anxious about the meaning that all his thoughts, words and deeds amount to in the face of death, but unable to resolve decisively on any particular way of giving meaning to his life as a whole. This is the typical predicament of what Heidegger calls the 'inauthentic' life of the modern world, and it is fairly obvious that a person immersed in such a life, with no overarching sense of purpose, will not be able to say much about the meaning of Being. The metaphysical concern for 'Being', indeed, has dissolved into the multiplicity of concerns we have for particular, finite beings.

If we want to know about Being, then, we will have to find someone else, someone who is no longer in the grasp of inauthentic life but has become authentic. Such a one would speak only the words he speaks from the depths of conviction and understanding (and would therefore probably speak very little); he would gather the fragmentary meanings dispersed through time and scattered about in the 'chatter' of social talk into a unified vision and purpose, resolutely affirming his own meaning in an unblinking confrontation with death.

Where can we find such a one? Heidegger is, of course, much too modest to claim to be a representative of such authenticity himself. The furthest he goes in *Being and Time* is simply to say that *if* we are to become able once more to ask the question of Being, we must first lift ourselves out of the typical modern state of distractedness and mediocrity. But this means that the philosophical question of Being actually depends on life-decisions taken outside the realm of philsophy as such, decisions that seem to have more in common with will than knowledge. Yet can we will our way towards Being?

Heidegger himself is clearly embarrassed at this point, and later claims not to have meant any such thing in *Being and Time*, because he can see that such a reliance on will[8] is no better placed than revelation or mysticism to provide a satisfactory way out of the ontological impasse. For the fraternity of authentic human beings would necessarily be a secret society. They have no distinguishing marks, and their characteristic resolve is not communicable in language. We have no way of distinguishing between the person who says 'I am authentically resolved' and knows not what he says, and the person who says the same thing but really is so resolved. The truth of such authentic resolve is known only to the authentic person himself and is not a matter of public knowledge or scrutiny. It is, as Heidegger, says, cloaked in reticence. Like religion, it becomes a private matter. But once this is conceded (and Heidegger does concede it), the one who is authentically resolute must disown any claim to be able to offer knowledge of Being to others, since public knowledge cannot admit of esoteric sources that are the exclusive preserve of cognitive minorities. If knowledge cannot be demonstrated to be such to any reasonable person of good will, it is not knowledge. As Wittgenstein said, there is no such thing as a private language – but that, it seems, is the only language that the authentic ones can speak.

Later in his career Heidegger turned away from his earlier emphasis on authenticity and resolve and became preoccupied with poetry. He saw great poetry, along with the foundational words of the earliest Greek philosophers (which were themselves still poetic words), as enshrining an original plenitude of meaning that could put us in touch once more with Being. Again, however, his project

---

[8] The term is inadequate, but indicates the kind of emphasis that many of Heidegger's first readers heard in his work.

stumbled over the problem of how the essentially qualitative language of poetry could be made meaningful in a public domain dominated by the call for systematic clarity, consistency and verifiability. Like revelationism and mysticism, Heidegger too seems to succumb to a strategy of withdrawal from the realm of public knowledge.

Heidegger, of course, is a philosopher and not a theologian, and it might be objected that the 'failure' of his philosophical venture (a failure that became the starting-point for postmodern philosophy) has no special significance for theology. However, apart from the fact that for many years in the middle of the twentieth century theology was in the grip of a debate as to how far it should 'existentialize' itself (that is, remodel itself on the basis of Heidegger's philosophy), Heidegger's failure is important as marking the last large-scale attempt to revivify metaphysics and to give back to philosophy a sense for the question of Being. In this attempt philosophy, no less than theology, found itself having to appeal to esoteric experiences that turned the public discourse of knowledge into an essentially private language.

The result is not simply to confirm theology's dethronement as Queen of the sciences; it is to declare an intellectual republic in which there is no sovereign science, no single universal, all-encompassing meta-science that prescribes to each particular science its limits. To proclaim the end of theology, then, is not to engage in an act of spite against theologians. It is simply to declare that, whatever we may mean by the term today, theology can no longer make good the claim implied by its own name, taken in the strictest sense, that is the claim to speak truthfully about what is Really Real. If theologians are happy to redefine their work in terms of one or other human science (and it is striking how far, for example, literature and social science have set the agenda for much of the most interesting theology in recent years), that is well and good. But is it still *theology*?

We shall return to these questions, but first we should notice one more point.

The tradition of metaphysical philosophy that Heidegger attempted to reinterpret and relaunch is, of course, only one strand in the complex circuitry of contemporary knowledge. As well as the so-called 'continental' philosophy, there are the schools of Anglo-American philosophy, which have, superficially at least, set themselves a very different set of tasks. Here the focus is far more on the interface between philosophy and 'serious' science, and the aim is not so much to demarcate a dimension of qualitative thinking into which science can never trespass as to stimulate the scientific project itself into an ever more careful description of its own objectives and results. Here the philosopher, though still critical, is more of a fellow-worker with the scientist, rather than a poetic or prophetic opponent critic.

In this context, the *de facto* power of science to decide for us what counts as really real (n.b., no capital letters are now needed!) is ever more firmly secured. If it has not yet been proven that mind is reducible to brain, and thought to electro-chemical processes that are themselves managed by genetically installed controls, it is the ever-widening frontiers of science that determine the ever-narrowing frontiers of philosophy, and not *vice versa*. However, science itself is no single, unitary discipline or ideology but a complex of interdependent research methods and results. The really real, then, is itself no longer a single entity, but the best result of the best research to date across a multiplicity of fronts. If we want to know about it, we have to get into the detail. The work is done in the engine-room, not the bridge.

The theologian is not alone. No one has a view from above any more. But the question then arises as to whether, in this situation, it is still possible to go on thinking about God, and, if so, what such thinking would be like.

2

From Void to Dialogue

The principle of dialogue

The conclusion of the previous chapter might seem purely negative, in so far as it seemed to end by saying that neither theology nor philosophy nor any other science was both able and willing to answer the question what Being really is. As a consequence, all interpretations of the meaning of life, the world and the universe seem to be left hanging in an ontological void. All we can say is what contemporary science tells us we can say, namely, what works, what can be predicted and what can be manipulated. We cannot even begin to answer the eternal questions: what is true? what is it all for? what does it all mean? – And maybe we don't even know how to formulate the questions properly.

Is the outcome, then, nihilism of one kind or another – the despairing nihilism of existentialism, the jesting nihilism of postmodernity or the practical nihilism of science and technology?

Many have posed the question facing us in just these terms – and this is something religious apologists are especially likely to do – assuming that if knowledge of ultimate reality eludes us, then all we are left with is the void of nihilism. But is that so? Is renouncing the ambition of constructing or defending an overarching metaphysical framework the same as saying that we have *no* important or profound resources for giving meaning to life, for debating truth, or for acting justly? Is it really a question of all or nothing? And even if it is, must we understand 'nothing' in terms of blank emptiness, the outcome of an irreversible intellectual entropy? After all, for Christian theology 'nothing' is that from which creation was brought forth by God's creative word in the beginning, whilst Buddhists can speak of nothingness as the womb from which the interconnected web of life springs into existence.

Consideration of such questions will be fundamentally influenced by some basic assumptions about the nature of religious and philosophical thinking. Until relatively recently, it was generally assumed that although (for example) Hume might have been a greater prose writer than (say) Locke, or Newman than Maurice, the literary manner of a serious theological or philosophical work was secondary to the coherence and cogency of its arguments. Elegant periods were no substitute for clear logic or persuasive evidence. Nor should we too easily let slip this long-held bias in favour of substance over against the contemporary cult of style. Not insignificantly, much of the present disenchantment with politics has to do with politicians' obsession with 'presentation' and their (apparent) belief that voters will be won over if only policy is presented in the right light. It rarely seems to be acknowledged that some policies actually can have a serious impact upon the way in which voters live, and that public dissatisfaction with certain policies might just be to do with the fact that that impact is experienced as unacceptable, no matter what 'spin' is put on it. It is not my intention now to follow where the spin doctors have led. All the same, it is still possible to argue that the force and persuasiveness of any particular truth or doctrine will often be inseparable from the way in which it is expressed. Style cannot replace substance, but often the substance is revealed most clearly in the style. Revealed – and, perhaps, betrayed, since style can often tell us things about an author's or an institution's aims and commitments that are not acknowledged in the surface grammar of its self-presentation. Style can therefore provide a clue that takes us to the very heart of the issues themselves. The rhetorical style of postmodernity, for example, with its ceaseless hypostatization of abstract nouns and its hyphenation of familiar philosophical terms (thereby rendering the familiar unfamiliar), together with its characteristic vocabulary of 'violence', 'transgression', 'other-ness'/'alterity', 'diremption' and 'difference' (or -ance), already signals the intention of those who use it to distance themselves from any claims to direct acquaintance with 'reality' and to break from what they regard as the received wisdom and dominant discourse of the tradition.

In looking for possibilities of thinking about God 'after meta-physics' (to use an expression that has, by now, become somewhat clichéd), I want, then, to begin with a category that could be understood as having more to do with the form or style of thinking than with any particular content. In particular, I should like to focus on the distinction between monological and dialogical styles of thought and expression. This distinction cuts right across many of the traditional distinctions used by philosophers and theologians to classify systems of belief or world-views, distinctions such as those between idealism and realism, between knowledge and will, and between reason and revelation.

Whereas monological idealists will eternally confront monologi-cal realists in a static and sterile stand-off, dialogically-motivated idealists and dialogically-motivated realists will be able to speak to one another fruitfully, and with some excitement, without necessa-rily reaching agreement. Each may nurture the hope of winning the other round, but will also recognize that there are many useful things to achieve in terms of clarification and understanding that fall short of out-and-out victory. Similarly, those who espouse revelation or the narratives of scripture and tradition as the exclusive sources and criteria of right Christian belief may do so monologically (and often do) – but they don't have to (and often don't). Indeed, it would not be hard to argue that the biblical text itself, because of the kind of text it is, welcomes a dialogical reading.

This may seem a surprising claim, since our culture abounds in powerful stereotypes of the Bible being invoked monologically, as in 'Bible-thumping'. To those under the influence of such stereotypes, it will be virtually impossible to read or to hear the Bible as anything other than dogmatic in the worst sense of the word: exclusive, authoritarian, didactic and legalistic. If we are capable of putting the stereotypes aside, however, a very different picture emerges. In this picture the Bible is itself profoundly dialogical, constantly arguing with itself, constantly presenting diverse and shifting perspectives on the ongoing and multi-faceted debate between God and humanity. Such a dialogical reading might, for example, look more to the Abraham who argues (successfully) with God about the destruction of Sodom and Gomorrah than to the Abraham who unquestioningly agrees to sacrifice Isaac, and it might look more to the Job who maintains his cause and protests his innocence to the verge of blasphemy than to the patient Job of pious legend (who is, in fact, scarcely to be found in the biblical text itself). Again, a dialogical approach to the Bible would not only want to draw attention to the clear difference in tone between, say, the Book of Ecclesiastes and the prophetic writings, but would also respect the kind of internal argument between the writer and God to be found in Jeremiah no less than in Ecclesiastes. Even within the narrower compass of the New Testament, the dialogical reader would observe the tension between some of the words of Jesus and some of the claims ascribed to him or made on his behalf by gospel and epistle writers. Similarly, due weight would be given to the different views of Saints Paul and James regarding the relationship between faith and works. It would be noticed that Paul has no single or simple view concerning the superiority of the New Israel over the Old, but is engaged in a passionate struggle to make sense of his double experience and double life as both Jew and Christian. For such dialogical readers none of these differences amount to contradictions that have to be ironed out or forced into some kind of more or less implausible harmony, because they do not share the prejudice that unity is privileged over diversity, monologue over dialogue.

To speak of the Bible as internally dialogical is, however, only a beginning. For genuine dialogue is never just internal; that is, it is never just a matter of an individual, a group or a text talking to itself. On the contrary, such internal dialogue only comes about as an aspect of or as a result of a larger exchange between self and world, self and other, one community and another. To continue with our example of the Bible. If we once start to become aware of the internal dialogue embodied in the pages of the biblical text, we will soon realize that this cannot be purely 'inter-textual'. For this internal dialogue is a reflex of the larger debate between Israel and its world. Israel did not generate its history, its beliefs and its Law out of itself, but came to be and to think and to practise those things that made it Israel in a vast, centuries-long process that interacted in many ways with the whole religious, political, economic and cultural life of the region. To be sure, this process often involved the sometimes violent suppression or repudiation of alternative perspectives, but even then the resulting position is inseparable from the fact that it demanded this particular act of repudiation and not another.

The point is essentially simple, and can be illustrated by reference to another complex of religious traditions: that of India. Early Buddhism expended considerable energy on defining itself over against the dominant Hindu culture in which it developed. One of the primary issues involved its attitude towards the view that salvation could be achieved through heroic feats of asceticism, involving fearsome disciplines of mind and body. Such a question, however, was more or less completely irrelevant to Israel and, largely, to early Christianity (although it did become important in the later history of the church). It was simply not an issue. What was an issue was, for example, how to survive as a small community surrounded by larger and often hostile imperial powers, or how to re-establish communal identity in the wake of a national humiliation that culminated in exile, or how to adapt the mores of a nomadic people to agrarian and, later, urban life – and it is in response to such challenges that the characteristic 'faith of Israel' acquires its unique shape. This is not to reduce that faith to its environment, a temptation that influenced an

earlier generation of scholarship when new archaeological discoveries revealed for the first time the extent of the overlap
between Israel and its neighbours. It is simply to say that we
cannot tear the faith of Israel out of its context, and the fuller our
knowledge of that context, the fuller our understanding of the
faith. Naturally, the task involved in expanding such knowledge is
potentially limitless, and some might argue that it is a task of
merely scholarly curiosity with no bearing on the actual living
out of the religious life: the religious life, it is said, has a quality
of urgency that cannot wait on the outcome of such endless
investigations. Of course. But again that is a problem only for
those who have already subscribed to a monological approach. If I
am a dialogical believer, I know that my present state of knowledge is imperfect and incomplete, but that does not inhibit me
from offering the best interpretation I can of what is available to
me, and being prepared to apply that interpretation as best as I
can in my own circumstances.

These last comments point to a further dimension of the
dialogical point of view. In reading the Bible dialogically, I am
never simply concerned with drawing attention to the internal
dialogicality of the text, nor even with establishing lines of debate
and dialogue between the text and its context. I am also concerned
by the fact that my present world is not, at least not in any
immediate or simple sense, the world of the Bible. If I am to talk
about the 'meaning' of the biblical word, then, I will have to
establish lines of dialogue connecting my world to that of the Bible,
and the world of the Bible to the world I inhabit. In this respect,
dialogue always involves a certain tension. On the one hand, it
means establishing links between past and present. On the other, it
means respecting the distance between them. For even though
dialogue necessarily seeks points of contact, it instinctively shuns
over-hasty acts of identification. I cannot collapse the distance
separating the past from the present. The first and the twenty-first
centuries are divided by precisely twenty centuries, twenty
centuries of continual and colossal change. The person who speaks

in the one cannot be heard by the person who inhabits the other without the help of an interpreter. The past is not another world, but it is another country.

The preceding remarks may seem to have been targeted exclusively at undermining a particular conservative, biblicist kind of monologism. However, it should be said as clearly as possible that that is only one brand of monologism, and its liberal and radical opponents are equally capable of manifesting monological tendencies of an extreme kind. Although their positions differ absolutely in terms of content from those of conservative believers, they are often no less simplistic, one-sided and exclusive.

We can see this by turning back to some of the founders of radical religious thought in the nineteenth century, thinkers like Ludwig Feuerbach. Feuerbach demonstrated to the satisfaction of many that religion in general and Christianity in particular was 'nothing but' the result of human beings having invested their highest goals and values in an illusory supreme being. The secret of theology, he insisted, was anthropology. What needed to be done was to withdraw our investments from their illusory object (God) and re-invest them in ourselves. Instead of living and working for the glory of God, we should live and work for the glory of Man, devoting ourselves to creating a harmonious, humanist society on earth. In this society reason would provide a way of fulfilling ancient religious longings: science would turn the desert into a land flowing with milk and honey, free love would do away with the selfishness of marriage, and a belief in humanity would undermine historically-conditioned differences between classes and nations.

There is undeniably much that is attractive about Feuerbach's vision, but there is also a darker side, a side revealed in the way in which these ideas were taken up and transformed by the revolutionary left in Russia. That which had no real existence according to the theory should not exist in society, and if it did exist, it was to be abolished. The logic of the Communist attempt to give history a helping hand by wiping religion out before it could fully wither away is already contained in Feuerbach's philosophical agenda.

Now it would be absurd to claim that those radical theologians of the twentieth century who have followed the trail blazed by Feuerbach intended to give aid and comfort to the totalitarian application of his ideas. Nor am I primarily concerned here with the political consequences of ideas, but with the nature of the ideas themselves. But this is precisely where the after-life of Feuerbach's philosophy in Russian Communism is so interesting, for even if the Bolsheviks' application of his ideas can be portrayed as perverting them, it nonetheless highlights something about the ideas them-selves: their characteristic exclusiveness. It is not inappropriate to call Feuerbach's approach to religion reductionist, because what he sought to do was precisely to reduce religion to its simplest elements. That is why the refrain 'Such-and-such a doctrine is *nothing but . . .*' is heard again and again throughout his critique of Christianity. Baptism is *nothing but* an affirmation of the value of water, the eucharist is *nothing but* a celebration of the value of eating, etc. Where Feuerbach led, others followed: Marx, Nietzsche and Freud, the so-called 'masters of suspicion' who did so much to create the ideological climate of our own time in which it is so widely assumed that religion is *nothing but* the reflection of some social, psychological or intellectual malaise, unrecognized by believers themselves (who are thus represented as a species of half-wits, who know not what they do).

It is one of the more curious twists in the tale of the history of ideas that this tactic of reductionism was eventually taken up by some theologians. As it became clearer that modern theology had to face up to what I have called the demise of ontology, it became attractive to some to seek to reformulate the aims and principles of theology in ways reminiscent of Feuerbach. Theology, it was now said, is not about heaven but about earth; religious language is not other-worldly but this-worldly; the Christian concern is not with the sacred, but with the secular. Now, however, reductionism was not being used to attack religion, but as an intellectual legitimation for carrying on being religious in a situation in which revelation and metaphysics no longer carried conviction. First came the attempt to demythologize the New Testament, and to recast the meaning of the New Testament myths in terms of the struggle for existential authenticity. Then came the 'theology of the death of God' and the 'secular theology' of the 1960s, and other reductionist forms of revisionism have followed in their wake. As a gesture against dogmatic immobility in the face of the challenge posed by modernity, such theologies may command some sympathy and, as stop-gaps, perhaps they can also provide temporary oases for the spirit. The problem is that they tend to perpetuate the exclusive, negative, reductive gesture of the nineteenth century's humanist attacks on religion. Typically their slogans declare that 'We can no longer think that . . . or say that . . . or believe that . . .' Their concern seems to be more to do with erecting 'No Entry' signs on roads that have become impassible than with pointing towards whatever possibilities and openings are to be found within the new situation itself. Paradoxically, however, this approach only buries theology still deeper in the grave of metaphysics, since it is defining itself (albeit negatively) in relation to beliefs concerning what is or isn't the case. The logic is that of the metaphysician: that religious language can only operate in the territory of the really real, as that is described by the best available form of knowledge – only today that form is no longer metaphysics, but science.

That, however, is to make a presumption about the nature of the real, from which dialogical thought refrains.[1]

It is easy to see that dialogue, as envisaged here, is never going to be simple. It is not just a matter of switching from metaphysical to postmodern mode, since dialogue is in principle never-ending and

---

[1] Some might feel that I am also accepting the reductionist case and availing myself of its characteristic rhetoric of negation when I insist on 'the end of theology' as conceived metaphysically. However, as I have already argued, dialogicality is not just a matter of surface grammar, but of style. The question is whether the opponent's view or position is simply negated without a hearing, or whether it is engaged with in such a way as to show respect for its manner of questioning and asserting. Naturally an author cannot offer guarantees as to whether he has succeeded in doing that.

open-ended. Genuine dialogue, like love, never comes to an end. Any 'conclusion' it may arrive at is and can only ever be provisional.

If dialogical thought thus takes up an attitude of openness towards its own future, it is no less open towards its past. If it is part of the rhetorical armoury of ideologies of modernism and postmodernism to trump their opponents by claiming to speak in the name of the newest and latest critical perspective,[2] dialogism has no such pretensions. On the contrary, it is more than happy to acknowledge its debt to a long line of thinkers (in the twentieth century, one might think of Martin Buber, Gabriel Marcel and Mikhail Bakhtin) who have espoused and expounded a dialogical view of life. If, as I have argued, the Bible is itself a dialogical text, it is scarcely surprising that many representatives of Jewish and Christian traditions are drawn towards dialogism. However, it is also in the nature of the case that dialogical thought can only with difficulty and distortion be pressed into the mould of a school or programme, and dialogism has never spawned a cohesive movement as have neo-orthodox or existentialist theologies. This has again to do with the fact that dialogicality is as much a matter of form or style as of content.

But it is not just the biblical sources of Western civilization that have given an impulse to dialogical thinking. The Hellenic sources of our culture have also played their part. Here, for example, we find the principle of dialogue enshrined in the very form of philosophy's defining texts, Plato's *Dialogues*, and, no less importantly, in the works of the great Greek dramatists who have continued to inspire both literature and philosophy.

The reference to Plato's *Dialogues*, however, forces us to be a bit

---

[2] Thus the penchant for the prefix 'post-', which immediately positions the viewpoint being proposed (postmodern, postfeminist, postliberal, etc.) as being more genuinely contemporary than those it is 'post-' (modernists, feminists, liberals, etc.) and therefore, in some unexplained sense, inherently superior. Ironically, the rhetorical trick being played here is nothing if not modernist.

more precise as to just what is meant by the dialogical principle. Many readers of these *Dialogues* have had a sense that, to put it crudely, the 'dialogue' element in them is phoney. Like a barrister conducting a cross-examination, Socrates seems to know just where he wants to get to by pursuing a particular line of questioning, harrying and confusing his interlocutor as he goes, and his own expressions of bewilderment and self-irony often seem to be purely rhetorical. If that is true, then the 'dialogue' form of Plato's philosophy is just that, a mere form used to convey a teaching that is true in itself, whether or not it is expressed dialogically. It is, in other words, what Buddhists might call a case of 'skilful means', a way of adapting the teaching to the situation and understanding of the learner: wonderful pedagogy, but not significant in itself with regard to the content of what is being taught. To put it another way: dialogue here has come to mean dialectic, a methodical means to a predetermined end. All the humour and poetry of Plato's work cannot, at the end of the day, disguise the fact that, as in Hegel, this dialectic is a matter of remorseless logic, in which the passions and interests of the participants have a purely accidental relation to the eventual outcome.[3]

Whether these charges can be made to stick in the case of Plato is not my present concern. My point is rather to draw attention to the fact that the real dialogical character of a text is never just a matter of its outward form. Irrespective of Plato, it is certainly true that there are many 'dialogues' in the history of philosophy that are no more than thinly-veiled monologues. Conversely, there are many first- or third-person works that are powerfully dialogical, works like Augustine's *Confessions*, in which the writer exposes not only the passionate dialogue between himself and God, but his own

---

[3] This is not, of course, an appropriate context in which to broach the question as to how far Plato's Socrates faithfully represents the historical Socrates. It may well be that Socrates himself was more open-ended. Also we have to acknowledge that even some of Plato's own *Dialogues* fail to reach a conclusion, and cannot therefore be accused of imposing closure on their subject-matter.

inner perplexities. It is striking how, in such a supposedly 'monological' text in which only one voice, Augustine's, actually speaks, questions are left open and unresolved.[4]

Thorough-going dialogism is always resistant to pre-emptive closure. But it does not follow that those who embrace dialogism are sceptics or uncommitted. It is rather that, committed as they are, they recognize that the point of view they seek to represent and promote cannot be realized apart from the process of dialogue. As the dialogical thinker sees it, meaning is not something to be reached or established by reductively tracing the manifold beings and expressions back to abstract first principles or to some simple primordial experience. It is instead seen as all the more meaningful, the more it is enriched by the accumulation of perspectives and experiences brought to it by the other participants in the dialogical process. Consultation is not simply a political gesture, aimed at getting agreement for a position already decided upon; it is itself integral to the emerging nature of the truth, theoretically as well as practically. Perhaps remembering that the grandest-ever piece of human engineering, the Great Wall of China, was not built by starting from one end and continuing to the other but by beginning from a number of different points, dialogism puts itself in the position of never being able to give a single, simple answer to the question where it began or where it is likely to finish. But it is not embarrassed by this perplexity. On the contrary, it recognizes that this is just as it should be.

It has been said that Hegel transformed the way we think, by getting philosophy to take history seriously. His system was not like previous logical systems that aimed to construct a timeless and unchanging body of laws of thought. In his hands, the philosopher became more like a novelist, telling the story of how Spirit grew to self-consciousness and, as it were, became a man – just like the genre of 'novels of education' popular in his day. Dialogism goes

---

[4] Curiously, when Augustine wrote treatises in the literary form of the dialogue, the result is often profoundly monological!

further, however. It is not just about telling the story of a single hero, or presenting the unfolding of a single point of view. It is more like a drama than a novel, for it allows the simultaneous presence of a number of diverse voices that cannot necessarily be synthesized into a unitary whole. It is, moreover, a drama of a radical and inventive kind, since it is one that necessarily involves the spectator. In so far as it claims that dialogue is itself the ultimate principle of philosophy, dialogism implies that truth is not the kind of thing that can ever be established without our active involvement.

An agenda for dialogue

But, it might be objected (and theologians may well be amongst the first to object), isn't this at the end of the day just a recipe for talk, talk and more talk? What is all this dialogue actually *about*? What is its aim and purpose? Where is it going? Where is its energy? And what about those of us who don't have time for dialogue because we've got things to do in the world, deeds great and small awaiting us?

The tone of irritation contained in such questions is certainly justified if dialogism is nothing more than the self-justifying ideology of armchair thinkers. But that, I contend, is not the case. The principle of dialogue is inseparable from both a theoretical and a practical engagement with what have been called our ultimate concerns.

One answer to the question as to what dialogue is *about* is simply that it is indeed about dialogue itself. In a world racked by one violent crisis after another, where a multiplicity of conflicting ideologies face each other within a rapidly shrinking global village, dialogue is the way of co-existence. My first duty to my neighbour is not to convert or to coerce him, but to talk to him. As long as we keep talking, we are not at war. Seen in these terms, a philosophy of dialogue might be construed as the theoretical expression of a UN view of the world. And perhaps we could extend this by suggesting that dialogue is democracy, and that the larger the number of people talking to each other about the largest possible number of issues, the more likely it is that conflict will be deferred. And even if none of the voices ever get just what they want, everybody gets something, even if they only get heard.

That a philosophy of dialogue is fitted to serve as a philosophy for our time might seem to be strengthened by such considerations. For if our intellectual situation is, as I have claimed, conditioned by the occurrence of an ontological vacuum into which the grand narratives of philosophy and religion are now imploding, and if, as a consequence, no single position or point of view can go on claiming any kind of unique privilege, we simply have to take others as seriously as we take ourselves. The imperative of dialogue in the service of co-existence and a first step to consensus is, it might be said, as necessary in the sphere of theory as it is in that of social, economic and political life.

UN diplomacy and democracy are, very probably, good things, or at least less bad than many of the alternatives currently on offer. But the principle of dialogue being advanced here is not primarily modelled on political analogies, even if it may turn out to have political implications.[5] More important is the fundamental reciprocity between the principle of dialogue and the principle of personality.

What gets revealed by the dialogical process (and in this respect it doesn't immediately matter what the particular point at issue may be) is the richness and complexity of the self's interconnectedness with others and with the world, and, as a kind of reflex of this, the richness and complexity of the self's inner self-relatedness. In the discovery that no one is an island – a discovery renewed in every real act of dialogue – we simultaneously discover that the self is not a single, indivisible unit. Self-relation and world-relation are inseparably interconnected. The person who has no world has no

---

[5] See my concluding comments in the section 'Towards the Ethical' in Chapter 5 below.

self, and the person with no self has no world. Every time the world reveals a new aspect of itself to me, I learn something new about myself. Every time I experience a new power or dimension within myself, I realize that the world contains more things than my philosophy had hitherto dreamed of. Self-sufficiency is a principle that may have some important applications in economic or psychological life, if understood in a very rough and ready way, but as an aim or principle it is radically incoherent. There is and can be no such thing, in either the moral, the intellectual or the personal sphere.

When Descartes said 'I think therefore I am', he identified consciousness with the act of the first-person-singular subject. But what if consciousness is more like the reflection in the 'I' of the other 'I', that is, in turn a reflection of another 'I': a situation perhaps best envisaged by analogy with the lovers who, looking into each others' eyes, discover what each means to the other, finding themselves in and through the other? One thing, of course, leads to another, and it is the most widely acknowledged of all truths (apart from the truth that each of us must die) that we came into the world via a foetal stage of existence in which we were entirely dependent for our life on the life of our mother, and that the most basic building blocks of our 'personality' are shaped in the early months of our lives by the way in which (usually) our mothers and other close relatives physically, emotionally and verbally draw us into the network of social relationships in which we become who we are. If the 'I' comes to be a separate thing for itself, it is and can only be on the basis of this primary socialization. We are, it may be said, loved into selfhood. The biological and psychological root of dialogue is in the infant drawing its nourishment from the body of another and, in doing so, fulfilling the need of the other to give nurture. This process is next sublimated into the language of facial expression, before rising to language itself. We are not only not islands, we never were. We will be only in death, if then.

A similar picture emerges when we move to the level of thought. For truth itself is never truth in isolation. Truth is what it is only in and by means of its connection to other truths. The basic logic of true statements, '*x* is *y*', is empty unless the two terms, *x* and *y*, are in at least one respect distinct and therefore susceptible of being related. The ambition of idealist philosophers to deduce the whole of existence from the simple self-evidence of the tautologous principle *A=A* was a crazy aberration, a wild gamble in the face of the sudden expansion and complexification of knowledge in the early modern era.

However, dialogism is less concerned by such abstract considerations than by the thought that truth is always truth spoken or expressed by someone. All sorts of things may be true, in some sense, but if no one knows of them, it is very hard to know what their being true can mean. Augustine says somewhere that if the world ceased to exist, it would still be true that the world didn't exist, thereby demonstrating, to his own satisfaction at least, the objectivity and transcendence of truth (Truth with a capital 'T'!). Dialogism takes the opposite view: it is only when there are people concerned to assert truths that we can speak of truth at all. Persons are the primary agents of dialogue, and the question of the truths asserted by persons is only a preliminary to the question of the truth of personality itself. What dialogue ultimately reveals, then, is nothing other than the truth of the person. But that is not to say that the person is the 'object' of dialogue, the end to which the dialogue is merely the means. For, as I have suggested, the person doesn't exist outside the social process of which dialogue is the articulation. It is not by means of dialogue but *in* dialogue itself that I get to know who I am and who you are, and I 'know' this only in so far as I remain within the movement of dialogue. Neither an instrument nor a method, dialogue is a style that discloses substance[6] – and the substance that dialogue discloses is none other than that of the person.

It is in its defining interconnection with this personal dimension

---

[6] I am using the term 'substance' here in a popular, not a philosophical sense.

of truth that dialogism is, I suggest, best seen as a pressing requirement for contemporary thought about the human condition and, my particular concern in these pages, contemporary thinking about God. Let me say what I mean by this.

The mystery of personality

In the previous chapter, I traced the tale oft-told of the decline of metaphysics and the inversely correlated advance of science and the secular. For many people today, including many who rarely think about such things for more than five minutes at a time, the world in which we live is a world that could be described as built on Stephen Hawking's mathematically-ordered universe, peopled by Richard Dawkins' selfish genes and understood by Stephen Pinker's computer-like consciousnesses. In other words, it is a world in which life, including human life, is nothing but the product of blind, impersonal, purposeless but predictable forces. Even if the acclaimed anthropic principle assures us that the world is none-theless such as to have produced minds like ours, we are but little comforted. Mind, thought, value (or, if one likes beauty, truth and goodness) have no reality in themselves. They are ripples on the surface of cosmic becoming, no more. The fact that many of us carry on acting as if we believed that these things were built in to the nature of things (even, perhaps, as expressive of God's way of being present in the world, as its 'spiritual dimension') is simply a residue of pre-scientific thinking. Just as we continue to say 'the sun rises' despite the fact that we all know that it doesn't, we continue to use the vocabularies of metaphysics, morals and religion because, in a rough and ready way, they are adequate for our everyday purposes. But that doesn't mean that we hold them to be true, any more than, if pressed, we would say that 'the sun rises in the east' is an objectively true statement. That's how it seems to us – but it's not how it is.

When it comes to saying what *is*, what is really the case, really real, we defer to science, and, in the last resort to the science of such as Dawkins and Pinker.[7] Let theology accept this situation. Let thinkers and theologians bequeath to science what is left of the legacy of metaphysics, so that the 'real world' of metaphysics lives on in the 'real world' of science. In this 'real world', to repeat, our thoughts, values, personalities and spiritual stirrings have no 'real' status. These and similar terms are mere expressions of the 'seeming world', the world as it 'seems' to us to be, and we ourselves, as spiritual, value-adding beings, are just moments in the flux of this same 'seeming world'. 'I' am no metaphysical substance. 'I' have no Self with a capital 'S'. 'I' am no immortal soul. 'I', this 'being' that I am, is just a reflex of biological powers, a tiny humming in the gigantic cogs of the blind watchmaker's marvellous machine.

And yet.

And yet, I do 'seem' to myself to be something that is different from the sort of fact or the sort of event that can be the object of calculation and prediction. Even if I knew that there was already in existence a computer that could predict or simulate my every move and every thought – let's say a computer that could write this book that I am writing now – it matters to me that *I*'m doing it in a way it wouldn't matter to me if the computer were doing it. Indeed, if there were also a computer that could simulate your reading of this book – and that could even 'understand' it in some respects better than you are able to understand it – I would still be more interested in how *you* were reading it than I would be in how the computer

---

[7] Hawking, of course, plays his metaphysical cards too close to his chest for us to be absolutely sure whether he 'believes' in anything like a quality of transcendence that theology might be able to recognize as God. I once attended a lecture that was organized under the aegis of Hawking's College Chaplain and which was advertised in such a way as to encourage us to think that he was about to show his hand. However, the lecture began with him saying words to the following effect: 'If you've come here expecting to find out whether I believe in God, you're going to be disappointed.' Dawkins, of course, leaves us in no doubt! (Generally, it is often said, biologists and psychologists are more resistant to theology than cosmologists, physicists and mathematicians, but that's another story . . .)

was reading it: I would want to know what *you* think in a manner different in kind from the curiosity with which I would await a print-out of the computer's 'opinion'.

Now this again may be just a reflex, a case of what has been called biophilia, the affinity that living beings inevitably feel for each other. Perhaps a computer would be more interested in what another computer had written than in anything I could come up with. But even if a reductive explanation can (and it can) be applied in any case I could possibly imagine, it cannot get behind my concern for how the world seems to me. Even if I know better, it will for ever seem to me that my feelings, my ideas, my acts of moral evaluation and my personal commitments and relationships are *mine*, and are, indeed, *the most important things of all* to me, even if what they 'are', 'really', is not how they seem to me to be. They are what make up my life. If I were ever to write an autobiography, they would be of the essence of what I would write.

It is tempting to say that this sense of importance, the sense that what I experience as my life matters immeasurably – a sense inhering in the lived quality of life (whether I think about it or not) –, is something mysterious or obscure. Certainly, the scientific positivist and the hard-nosed analytic philosopher may want to label it in such terms, since they call 'mysterious' whatever can't be incorporated into their way of conceiving the world. But if it is mysterious, the mystery is of a very peculiar kind, since it is not something strange or far-off, something of which only a few rare or adventurous minds have experience, but the most everyday thing of all, present in all the great and small doings of my social world as well as in my private musings. Nor is it something I imagine to be my exclusive property. I have absolutely no doubt that you feel it in your case, just as keenly as I do in mine. In fact, I am fairly sure that a two-year-old has it in no less a measure, though no two-year-old could tell you about it in the way I'm trying to do now.

This peculiar, everyday mystery that I feel in every lived

moment of my life may be explicable in reductionist terms. It may be mere sentimentality, a reinvocation of the exploded pathetic fallacy, but even if I'm told all this it doesn't change the way I feel.

On the other hand, I am not wanting to establish the inescapable importance of such feelings as a base from which to launch some kind of counter-offensive against reductionism. Some modern philosophies and theologies have done just that, thinking to find in the sense of what Heidegger, for example, called 'mineness' a possible gateway to a renewal of ontology. I cannot claim to find in such feelings any grounds for ontological hope. I don't nurse the ambition of demonstrating that from these humble beginnings I can work my way up to a description of Being Itself or an account of what the world is 'really' like.

If dialogism thus understands itself as an agenda radically different from science, it does not follow that it is not interested in dialoguing with science also. The point is simply that this is not where it begins, nor does it wait upon the results of scientific enquiry or the possible completion of the realism v. non-realism debate. Because its procedure is shaped by a different set of considerations from those that mould the methodology of science, dialogical thinking about God is able to remain open to science. It neither derives from nor does it seek to dominate its scientific neighbours.

Because the dialogism I am wanting to explore has forsworn any claims to ontology, it has no particular line to push, either positive nor negative, about the ontological status of the feelings of 'mineness' I have invoked. It is concerned only with what they mean to me, the concrete person existing, now, in dialogue. Even if what I call 'my' life is only a so-called life, an illusion, then so be it. Then I *am* an illusory being – but this illusion is precisely what matters most of all to me: it is what I am for myself, and in myself.

A critical reader will by now have noticed something odd about the development of my argument. Whilst claiming to be promoting a philosophy of dialogue, I have been talking about I, me and mine, about the self or subject in its individual self-consciousness.[8] Where is the dialogue in all this? Isn't it all done in the manner of the purest of monologues?

Let me repeat a point already made: self-relation and world-relation are inseparably interconnected. If, in the face of the blind, impersonal, chaotic universe that popular science invokes to explain us to ourselves, I want to insist on the value of the personal, it is perhaps natural to begin with the closest and most intimate revelation of the personal I know, namely, the revelation of my own personhood. But although this is a convenient starting-point from the point of view of exposition, it is misleading if it is understood as excluding the other. My spontaneous sense that my personal life matters, and matters infinitely, is essentially the inner aspect of a bodily and social exchange. 'I' is itself a learned word, and my sense of personal value is brought into focus by my childhood nurture. Indeed, like most infants I probably called myself 'me' or 'George' (my given name) before I learned to say 'I'. In saying 'I' and in saying that 'I' matter, I am not simply asserting myself over against the world, I am responding to an opportunity that the world itself (chiefly in the form of my primary infancy carers) has opened up for me. Equally, in the very act of feeling that life, my life, matters, I am creating a focal point within the flow of energy from which, by expressing my feeling, I can redirect back to the world, specifically to the other persons with whom I immediately have to do, the value that I thereby affirm. If this sounds abstract and complex, it is in fact the most concrete and simple thing of all. As the mother gives to the child a sense of importance and being valued, so the child, even in the most spontaneous infantile response (a smile or a gurgle), gives back to the mother the love bestowed upon it, assuring her that she too in her act of loving is valued. Naturally,

---

[8] And, those who know about these things might add, I have used the thinly-disguised idioms of existentialism, the most subjective of all modern philosophies, a philosophy in which there is no room for genuine otherness and therefore no possibility of dialogue. Let us see.

many things can go wrong in real life, and such virtuous circles are not always to be found. Not all mothers or other primary carers are as loving as they should be, and some children seem frustratingly and inexplicably indifferent to the love bestowed upon them. The cycle of affirmation can be broken in many ways and set into reverse to become a cycle of destruction. To ignore this would be to paint a very simplistic and even sentimental view of the personal life. Yet even in its negative forms, the struggle for selfhood remains characteristically interactive. In asserting myself against the world and refusing the gift of love, I am the rebel I am only in relation to the world I am rejecting. In feeling myself alienated from the world, neglected, abandoned or even annihilated by it, it is precisely in relation to the world from which I am alienated or by which I have been abandoned that I feel my solitude most keenly. And 'the world' here is, of course, first and foremost the world constituted by other people.[9] Even if, with many poets and artists, I turn away from the human world to what we call nature, the chances are that I use nature as material for metaphor and simile by which to express my vision of the human and personal life.

It follows from this that philosophical debates as to whether the person should primarily be considered in terms of subjectivity or, instead, as standing under the claim of the world ('accused', perhaps, by it) can only ever achieve partial illumination of the full meaning of personality. It is of the character of personality that either perspective is in every case possible and, indeed, necessary if

---

[9] It would be tempting, but it would not be to my present purpose, to develop an extensive phenomenological description of the multiplicity of forms that the striving and the failing of the self-other relation can take. Not only the literature of existentialist writers from Kierkegaard to Sartre, but many of the great novels and dramas of the modern world, provide ways of exploring these forms – not to mention our own everyday experience. But although the consideration of concrete examples might further the persuasiveness of my argument, there are no examples that do not themselves require interpretation and that are not exposed to alternative readings. Having made the general point I therefore leave it to the reader's own experience and imagination to supply the examples.

we are to have the complete picture. But, of course, we never do get the complete picture. Even general comments such as these, comments recommending a balanced or complementary view of self and world polarities, are only general comments: they do not in themselves give us the complete picture they request. In the actual business of expounding and interpreting the meaning of personality we always have to submit to the hard discipline of leaving incomplete what is in fact unfinished. Precisely because it is only in and by means of the process of dialogue that the meaning of personality is revealed, we can approach this meaning only in so far as we ourselves remain *in* dialogue, and that means remaining in the tension of other-relatedness, offering our word and waiting upon a response, hearing the word of the other and reacting to it.

If this insistence on incompleteness seems to fall short of what some would regard as necessary for any truly persuasive view of the human condition (i.e., what I have called 'the complete picture'), the very existence of dialogue already marks a step out of the void into which, it seemed, the ambitions of metaphysics had collapsed. Dialogue cannot tell us what finally is the case or how things 'really' are. All it can do is to represent, to interpret and to reinterpret in demanding mutual honesty how the world seems to be. Like a spider's web in the process of construction, dialogue criss-crosses the empty space of the void with its lines of communication. If this web cannot embrace the totality of the world, we can be hopeful that it will catch the flies we need.

Once again, however, I can sense a certain impatience amongst my theological readers. 'This is not enough,' they are muttering. 'All this dialogue is no more than dialogue amongst human beings about human beings. What can it tell us of God?'

In the sense of metaphysics or of revelationism, the discipline of dialogue cannot, of course, tell us anything of God any more than it can tell us once and for all how the world is. Its aims are not ontological. But the theologians' question also invites a positive response. If the matter of dialogue is personality itself, it follows that the dialogist will want to say of God only what belongs to personality. In other words, dialogue approaches the question of God only with regard to the meaning of God in and for the personal life.

'There I have you!' The theologian jumps in. 'Your "thinking of God" is pure subjectivism, your "God" only a magnified image of your own self-absorbed preoccupation with yourself and the meaning your life has for you.'

Not so. For to say that God is personal is the most difficult thing we can say of God. It is, philosophically and religiously, more difficult than saying 'God is Being Itself' or 'God is the First Cause of the universe'. But if we want to speak of God in personal terms (and that, after all, would seem to be a minimum requirement of making any kind of sense at all of the Abrahamic faith traditions), we can do so only by means of a discourse that is itself fully personal. My case here is that only a truly dialogical discourse qualifies for this. It follows that whatever we (dialogically) think or say of God will be qualified by the essential incompleteness of all genuine dialogue, an incompleteness that is neither to be mis-interpreted as scepticism nor to be subjected to the siren voices calling for a renewal of ontology. If mysticism was critiqued in the previous chapter as being insufficient to found the public discourse of theology, we may nevertheless at this point appropriate the mystics' characteristic cry of 'Not yet!'. Whatever we can think or say of God is not yet the truth. In this way, the free and open yet infinitely difficult way of the person, dialogue makes its journey towards thinking about God.

One further important point belongs here. For what has just been said leaves open the question as to whether God is being thought of as, in some sense, identical with the human personality that discovers itself in and through dialogue, or whether God is 'another' person. Is the revelation of what some might call the 'True Self' identical with knowledge of God, or is the discovery of the True Self only the necessary (but perhaps insufficient) condition for venturing further out in search of God?

This is undoubtedly a question that has vexed previous philosophies of dialogue, and I do not pretend to be able to give a definitive answer. (To do so would, of course, falsify every word I have written in this chapter!) What can be said, however, is this: that whether or not we must finally reckon with the absolute transcendence of divine personality over human personality ('My ways are not your ways, says the Lord'), any way to God that seeks grounds of certainty outside a process of dialogue that, in the first instance, cannot be anything other than a human event, will be sub- rather than supra-personal. Even if it managed to come up with some items of genuine information about God, that information would be of no essential religious interest. But in the very nature of the case, we cannot prejudge what comes out of the dialogical process, and we will hesitate before claiming any 'results' that are anything other than provisional and in need of interpretation.[10]

At this point my sceptical theological interlocutor may be moved to repeat a previous objection. 'All this is all very well,' he splutters, 'but it's all talk. It's all at such a level of abstraction that I just don't know any more what you're talking *about*. There's no content to it. You dialogical thinkers are nothing but a collective of navel-gazers. What about those who don't have time to sit around enjoying such

---

[10] It will be clear to some readers that the kind of dialogism I am advocating differs in some important respects from that of Buber, perhaps the best-known exponent of dialogical thought in the twentieth century. Buber (and, for that matter, Marcel) seems to regard the encounter with the Other that lies at the root of the dialogical situation as being in some way charged with a kind of presence of God. What I am saying is that only the process of dialogue creates the conditions in which we can talk meaningfully about God, but the possibility of an 'encounter' with God, mediate or immediate, belongs to a future at which we have not yet arrived. 'God' is not a name for a reality that is already present in any definitive way, but for a possibility that first arises out of the process of seeking understanding on the path of dialogue. God is not a kind of pre- or sub-conscious stratum of my present consciousness. God is one whom I hope to address and be addressed by, to know as I am known – but not yet. All thinking about God must face up to the implications of this 'not yet', but although this is indeed already affirmed in general terms by many orthodoxies, it is far from obvious that they have thought through its implications.

amiably open-ended conversations? What about those oppressed by need and suffering, whose voices are never heard because society has stigmatized and excluded them in one way or another?'

The charge is fair in terms of what has been said so far. Furthermore, it points up a limitation in the term 'dialogue' itself. For 'dialogue' conjures up the impression of a group of socially equal, articulate interlocutors (somewhat like the participants at a Platonic banquet, perhaps, or a contemporary seminar or dinner party), fluent in self-expression and courteous in attending to others. In the so-called real world it is, of course, rarely like that. Power relations within groups and between groups distort the ideal speech situation of liberal discourse. Many, including the most needy, are excluded from the charmed circle and consigned to silence. And even when the privileged few do not themselves speak, they never lose their grip on the agenda.

I am not using the term 'dialogue' here, however, in such a way as to limit it to the ideal dialogical model. I am using it in a larger and looser, but also deeper and stronger, sense. For 'dialogue', as I understand it, does not only comprise the voices of those who know how to make themselves heard in the corridors of power; it also embraces all whose need is as yet unrecognized, unacknowledged, unheard but cries out for a hearing. 'Dialogue', in this sense, is not a product of culture or power, but the hope of the hopeless and the heart of a heartless world. The cry for justice is never just a cry for bread, though bread may be very necessary; it is also a cry to be recognized, acknowledged and heard, a cry to be seen as a person with all the rights, dignities and duties that go with that. Whether we are thinking of the abused child, the alienated adolescent, or the victims of war and poverty, the decisive issue is not whether we can address needs in an objective, technical way, but whether we are prepared to hear what those who have been insulted and injured by society want to say.

It is not the aim of this book to get involved with any particular area of social or moral concern. That does not mean that we can, in practice, think about God without some such rootedness in specifics. Indeed, part of what it means to say that dialogue is personal is that dialogue is always situated in a specific place and time. The dialogist is not interested in constructing a timeless schema of concepts and categories that are equally valid at all times and in all places. The dialogist seeks to understand what God means in this particular place and in this particular time, and that cannot be done without taking up particular moral and political commitments. 'Knowledge' is impossible apart from witnessing, in the sense of being committed to the truth that is affirmed. The concern of dialogue is not only with what I must say of God, but also with what, before God, I must do and how I am to be in relation to my neighbour.

Let us then attempt to give a local habitation and a name to the principles sketched in this chapter and explore the time and space of our contemporary attempt to think our way dialogically towards God. If in doing so we seem to pull back from the tough choices confronting us in the messy business of moral and political theologizing, this (it should now be clear) is not because these are regarded as unimportant, but because the theoretical orientation of the present work must inevitably leave open the detailed application of dialogical principles. At the same time I am convinced that it is precisely a dialogical understanding of religious thinking that best prevents us from immolating the passion of justice in the tomb of theory.

3

Tradition Against Traditionalism

The shock of the new

So far, I have only sketched the barest outlines of a post-metaphysical, dialogical model of thinking about God. As things stand, this could easily be portrayed as far too abstract and lacking in any real religious content. To be sure, I have argued that the implicit aim of dialogue is always directed towards the manifestation of the personal in its concrete fullness, and that this revelation is of itself enough to justify the dialogical process without any further apologies, additions or qualifications. Nonetheless, precisely because the personal only ever arises in and through the dynamics of interpersonal processes (including the elemental processes of birth and nurture as well as the refinements of philosophical and theological discourse), personality is known to us only as incarnated in, with and under the time- and space-bound conditions of biological and historical life. To say that the interdependent principles of dialogue and of personality are thus necessarily concrete is, however, still somewhat of an abstract statement. In this chapter and the next, then, I shall offer a preliminary orientation as to what I view as the more specific conditions that shape our contemporary thinking about God. I shall begin (in this chapter) by looking at the 'temporal' aspect of these conditions, i.e., the fact that we stand at a determinate historical juncture that both constrains and enables our thinking about God, and then continue (in the next chapter) by looking at the 'spatial' location of religious thought, particularly in terms of the institutional sites that provide the more obvious contexts in which such thought is pursued.

In doing so, I should at once acknowledge two important limitations on what I shall be saying. The first is the general point that although I hope to do enough to indicate what I regard as the most important factors conditioning contemporary thinking about God, a book such as this cannot hope to demonstrate the fullness of such thinking in its final concretion, since that would be nothing less than the totality of everything that belongs to the religious life of our times. All I can offer is a map or, more precisely, a set of directions that, with the help of the reader's own knowledge and imagination, might just succeed in showing the way I see this working out. It will therefore always be possible for an ill-disposed reader to complain that I have omitted one or other of the significant tendencies of contemporary God-think. I do not doubt that I shall be guilty of such omissions, since, for reasons already developed, I do not regard completeness as an achievable goal within theoretical work of this kind. Moreover, since pluralism, within and without the Christian churches, is one of the most striking characteristics of contemporary intellectual life, it is highly unlikely that any single study will be able to do justice to all the movements and trends of today's religious thought. Having forsworn the view from the bridge, it would be strange to proceed by trying to offer some kind of all-encompassing overview of where modern (or postmodern) thinking about God is at. Everything said here is necessarily caught in the tension between the general and the abstract on the one hand, and the particular on the other. Although my eye is on the particular, it can never quite reach it, and, to the extent that it draws close to it, it will lose sight of other particulars that are of burning concern elsewhere in the field of religious life and thought. I cannot, therefore, ever be altogether concrete across the board – but that is not my aim. My aim is less ambitious: merely to bring to the fore some of the key factors that, I believe, condition our aim to think God in the concreteness of social actuality.

The second limitation is, in a sense, a specific instance of the first. It is, simply, the limitation arising from the fact that my own view of the subject is that of a white male of middle-class origins and of middle age, writing from within one of the traditional centres of intellectual power and privilege and serving in the ordained ministry of a somewhat conservative established church. In terms of the theological developments of the last twenty or thirty years, this is not promising, since many of the most exciting and important of these developments have called into question the kind of hegemony over religious life and thought exercised in the past by individuals such as myself working in institutions such as King's College, Cambridge. The call for theology to become more contextual is repeatedly heard as a call to relocate theology away from the kind of bastions of privilege in which I live and work. This too, however, is a kind of context, even if it is one that some will dismiss as 'provincial'. Moreover, merely because contexts of this kind have played such a significant role – good or bad as the case may be – in shaping theology in the past, it does not follow that they should not be excluded in principle from the task of reshaping our contemporary thinking about God. On the contrary. Although those who seek to think about God in these erstwhile centres should no longer presume to dictate to others, because the history that they carry forward is itself one of the many factors conditioning our present intellectual situation, it needs to be represented within any reflection on that. Amongst the words of poetry most frequently quoted in modern philosophy are those of the German Romantic poet Hölderlin, 'Where danger is, there grows also the saving power' – and, if it is the case that the academic arm of established Christianity is one of the main culprits in infusing Christian thought with inappropriate metaphysical prejudices, perhaps that same arm must now be stretched out in the service of saving theology from itself: no longer leader or pioneer, but simply a colleague to those operating in quite diverse contexts, bringing diverse experiences to expression at the urging of equally diverse priorities.

'If I was going to *x*, I wouldn't start from here' is perhaps a sentiment felt by many caught up in the turbulent, often shapeless and directionless currents of contemporary religious thought. Maybe we would all like to be starting from somewhere else, but of course we all have to start from somewhere, and as a matter of fact we all do start from somewhere. In arguing the view that the human person is fundamentally 'dialogical', I alluded to the fact that we do not come into the world as self-created individuals but are, each of us, the product of reproduction, coming into being by means of the physical, psychological and cultural care and action of others. In terms of family and society, we inherit positive or negative possibilities and constraints that project the horizons of our future action, however indeterminately. As language users, we are initiated into languages that are already expansive and encompassing systems of communication, that we may add to or vary but never invent *ex nihilo*. Although meaning is something to be asserted and interpreted by each individual, the very possibility of meaning rests upon the existence of structures and systems that pre-date and circumscribe each particular individual. All this is alluded to in Heidegger's early insistence on what he evocatively called the 'thrownness' of human beings, indicating that we arrive in the world in the middle of a story long-since started, whose beginning is lost in the mists of the past and whose ending is hidden in the uncertainty of the future. Sartre, in his turn, spoke of the 'facticity' of the human condition, meaning that the sphere of human action is always inseparable from the utterly contingent and unrepeatable circumstances that accrue to us by virtue of our birth, upbringing and social and historical conditions.

These reflections are readily applicable to the task of thinking about God, since such thinking never occurs in a vacuum. The words and other public symbols of religion become available to us on the basis of the religious situation we inherit. We become religious by being taught forms of prayer, how to behave in church, Bible stories, and moral rules long before we appropriate their meaning for ourselves (a situation reflected in the institution of confirmation, in which young adults affirm on their own behalf their acceptance of the faith in which they have already been symbolically initiated by baptism). This observation not only supports the point that usage and practice precede understanding; it also indicates that the way in which we are religious always has the stamp of a particular local and historical situation. In the course of its expansion and internal differentiation, Christianity has generated a multiplicity of Christian cultures, such that one person will experience congregational hymn-singing and impassioned preaching as paradigmatic forms of religious behaviour, whilst another will think more in terms of weekly confession and mass-attendance. *This*, we believe, is what being religious means, the custom of our tribe. But this is not only true with regard to the general picture of religious belief and practice; it also applies to the narrower field of theoretical reflection on religion. The constellations of issues and ideas that provide the starting-point of the individual's and the generation's thought are, in the first instance, handed down from the past. In attempting to think about God, we find ourselves caught up in a conversation that predates (and, indeed, long predates) the moment when we first joined in. We therefore speak in the first instance with a vocabulary, with concepts and categories, in forms and on themes that are not our own. *Contra* Plato, it is not just a matter of drawing out a timeless, innate knowledge of God: whatever knowledge or understanding we arrive at is dependent on our having first been inducted into the greater conversation that precedes our arrival on the scene. Even when radical innovators break the mould of tradition, it is always a specific mould that is broken, and their new departures can never entirely slough off all traces of their origins. Proficiency in the received language is the precondition of understanding why and how it must be refuted or refused.

This lesson can easily be illustrated from within the history of religious thought. Martin Luther's insistence on faith is a specific response to the kind of emphasis on works prevailing in the church of his formative years, and his way of formulating the issue is inseparable from his own training and experience in the monastic culture of late mediaeval Europe. Had Luther not been a monk, he could never have broken the mould of medieval monasticism in the way that he did. Had he not zealously sought to practise the monastic vow of chastity, his marriage would never have had the symbolic force it did. Similarly, St Augustine's characteristic and epochal vision of Christianity would have been quite different if it did not internalize the specific contents of his wrestlings with Manicheeism and Platonism, wrestlings that took the form they did because of the cultural situation of Augustine's time. And so we could go on. The point is obvious to the point of banality – but it should not be overlooked. We all have to start somewhere, and we all have to accept that we will never entirely banish the circumstances of our beginnings from the further development of our thought. We have no need to be anxious that dialogue might ever lack material on which to go to work. The intellectual environment in which we first start to talk to one another is densely populated, and provides more than sufficient material for conversation.[1]

But this does not mean that we are subject to some kind of historical determinism. If the child is father to the man, the man is not simply a larger version of the child. Between the two lies a whole story of growth, choice and interaction with others. We are by no means limited to reciting the words and phrases that have been handed down to us from the past with more or less insight or power, nor are we constrained by the dominant agenda of our years of

---

[1] What is said here obviously goes some way towards providing a relative justification for the claims of the cultural-linguistic or narrative approach to doctrine. We do begin theologizing from within a particular community, taking our cue and our content from the historical deposit of that community's story as it has come down to us. But that is only one of the factors determining the shape of our thinking. None of us now lives entirely within the boundaries of any single community, and the sharpest provocation to serious thinking about God is precisely when our own experience or our exposure to the stories of alternative communities and traditions calls the story we have received into question. We may begin life within the protected world of home and family, but we can only gain maturity by stepping out of the family circle and engaging with the world on our own terms.

apprenticeship. We begin with what we have been given, but from the very beginning we ring the changes, incorporating our own experiences and experiments into the picture we have had bequeathed to us until, bit by bit, it becomes a new picture. Even if it is only all of a sudden that we notice that it has indeed become a new picture, the likelihood is that the final paradigm-shift will have been long-prepared by a history of gradual transformations, invisible fermentations and the accumulation of unrecognized pressures.

The radical who declares the dawn of a new age is only doing in an extreme form what every creative language-user does, and starts doing in earliest childhood. From the time we first begin to speak, we play with words and constructions, experimenting with different pronunciations and various expressive volumes and tones, juggling with words and constructions, building them up and knocking them down like wooden bricks, wilfully misapplying words and phrases or artfully re-applying them in new and surprising ways. Like so much else in childhood, this may seem like mere 'play', but is in fact by no means trivial: it is an integral part of equipping ourselves for our role as adult language-users. For language is not a cage or a rule-bound multi-dimensional game of chess. It may have game-like features, but it is also instrumental and communicative, a means by which I relate to the world and to those around me. I do not speak in order to enter into language, but my speaking is a purposive actualization of language. Once we have grasped this, we will be able to resist the seductive but often thoughtless fetishizing of 'Language' that has dogged much modern philosophy and theology. Language is not a self-contained universe, but is itself a dynamic element within a larger dynamic process. It is only one dimension amongst many of our human being. The fact that it can become self-referential, whether in the language-games of children or in the stylistic experiments of poets, does not lay down a prescription for the whole phenomenon of language. I use language *in order to* express, to assert, or to achieve something in the world. It may be getting a workman to place his building slabs in such-and-such a place, or it may be to persuade my beloved of the warmth and sincerity of my affections; it may be to coerce or to liberate others, to give voice to my feeling or to articulate philosophical understandings or to promulgate the laws of a nation – the possibilities are virtually endless. In every case there is a ceaseless interaction between the form of language and the context of its use. Language takes shape in and through the whole manner of our comportment towards our common world and, for this reason, is continuously being transformed (even if, in some cases, the transformation is extremely slow-moving).

Once again, religious thought provides ready examples. Take feminism, for instance. As it has developed over the last twenty-five years, one of the principle procedures of feminist theology has been to demonstrate how women had been rendered invisible within the theological mainstream by means of patterns of language-use inscribed so deeply into the skin of our culture that we take them to be 'natural' ways of speaking. The feminist revolt against such usages has been motivated by women's own experience and the gap or dissonance between that experience and the language available for its expression. This has been a constant stimulus to questioning and challenging the tradition and transforming contemporary practice. However, according to cultural-linguistic models of theology, such possibilities of radical revisionism and active, re-creative interventions in language-use ought not to occur. Against their view of things, I maintain that language is essentially unstable, always conditioned by context and essentially revisable and expandable.[2]

---

[2] It will be clear from this that I am very suspicious of Heidegger's attempt to philosophize by means of what he calls the 'basic words' of philosophy, words that, in their original Greek, are charged with a plenitude of meaning that is somehow resistant to depletion by time and changing cultural horizons – as long as we are able to hear them said as the Greeks said them. As I see it, we cannot tear individual words out of the whole complex of language-in-use in this way. The meaning of words is always provisional and always requires interpretation with an eye on the time and place of utterance. Vocabulary alone is meaningless apart from syntax, which in turn is embedded in larger linguistic and extra-linguistic structures and contexts.

The example of feminism also suggests another point. Not only is the language we use subject to change, but that change is of a certain specific kind. Changes in the theological language game are not just changes in forms of expression that leave the content of what is being expressed untouched. If, as I have claimed, the form of language constantly interacts with the use to which we put it (so that 'meaning' always involves both signifier and signified[3]), a change of form will always imply a change of content as well. Classical theoogical ways of understanding the occurrence of change in Christian doctrine invoke images like those of kernel and shell or seed and tree. If the former suggests an unchanging, timeless truth concealed behind a changing, historical form, the latter seems to allow for a more historical view, in so far as the seed itself changes as it becomes first a sapling and then a fully-grown tree. But even this image is too restricted, since there is a kind of direct, causal continuity between seed, sapling and tree that the extroverted dynamics of dialogically-determined change call into question. An acorn can only ever become an oak and a human baby can only ever become an adult human, but a conversation that begins by talking about one issue can finish by talking about something else entirely. Rather than thinking in terms of growth within the life-cycle of an individual representative of a species, we might do better to think of the kind of mutation explored by Darwin in his account of the origin of species, that is, the mutation from one species to another, the change by which a reptile becomes a mammal or a bird and a higher ape becomes human. In evolution we see a process in which radical and qualitative change is continually occurring, a process in which it is not so much a matter of the same 'types' putting on ever-new forms, but of a succession of types, interrelated, yet infinitely differentiated. So it

---

[3] This should not, of course, be read as implying that 'signifier' and 'signified' can be reduced to simple elements such that one word=one thing. On either side the structures of signification are complex, dynamic and interactive.

is, I suggest, with religion and religious thought. Unlike the nineteenth-century liberal view that sees the God of love as a refinement of the angry storm-God of Sinai, a refinement produced by shearing away that earlier God's local, primitive features and drawing out of the elements of personality and providential care hidden behind the wrathful visage, I would suggest that the emergence of the God of love from within the processes of historical change marks the occurrence of a genuine *novum*, a new thing, for which new words and new responses are demanded.[4]

Tradition

This *novum* is, once again, to be undertood with reference to the question of personality, since, whenever and however it comes into being, the quality of personality has the effect of radical novelty. Whenever we encounter the personal we find ourselves exclaiming with Shakespeare's Miranda, 'O brave new world that hath such creatures in it!' The revelation of the person is always experienced as the revelation of what eye has not seen nor ear heard nor the heart of man conceived. Personality is a fundamental feature of the realm of freedom and, as such, is irreducible to any system of causality and inexplicable in terms of any external factors. It is neither a result of a preceding chain of events, nor can it be used to predict a subsequent state of affairs.[5]

Nonetheless, everything that has been said so far warns us

---

[4] This might seem to be opening the way for the kind of supersessionist account of Jewish-Christian relations that would lead to expunging the Hebrew Bible (or large swathes of it) from the Christian canon. The further development of my argument should, however, make it clear that this is not what I am aiming at.

[5] Thus we cannot immediately use the specific historically-conditioned experiences and formulations of the New Testament community to bind subsequent thinking about God, nor yet to pass judgment on the preceding religious experience of Israel.

against projecting the irruption of the personal into a mystical realm of which we cannot speak and must keep silent. Precisely because I understand the personal as inseparable from the event of dialogue and therefore as inherently *inter*-personal, it will always be rooted in the particularity of the dialogical situation in which it emerges into the light of day. Love may make the world go round, but the experience of love is only ever given to us as the love of this particular person: it is these eyes, these hands, this voice that make the earth move under my feet and that change my world for ever. And if love, as it is said, always has a bitter-sweet quality, this is to do with the poignancy of staking the whole meaning of my life on the feelings aroused by these utterly contingent, utterly transitory externalities. Everything I love about the beloved is subject to the mutability that belongs to all flesh, and the mystery of love is precisely that of an encounter that elicits an absolute commitment in, with and under the conditions of inescapable impermanence. The supreme achievement of the greatest love poetry is therefore not to use the experience of love as a cipher or symbol in which to see some other dimension of timeless, eternal beauty; it is to see with the lover's eye why this beloved and no other has become love's unique occasion and inspiration. The experience of love does not make me want to talk or write about 'love'; it makes me want to talk or write about *her*. Beware of all lovers who are more interested in love than in the beloved!

The new, then, is always situated. It has its time and its place. It is an event occurring to these particular people in these particular circumstances that, by its occurence, charges their lives and times with a new significance, opening new possibilities of experiencing what the world means to them and what they mean for the world. In attempting to describe or interpret the *novum*, then, we have no resources other than those of historical experience itself. This is equally true when we are struggling to explain how we ourselves have entered into the mystery of freedom and when we are trying to trace the path of freedom in the world.

In fact, these two are intimately connected. The very aura of novelty that suffuses my experience of the personal calls into question the whole body of language and symbolism currently available to me. None of the words or images I have at my disposal will quite do. I am compelled to innovate. Yet my innovations will only make sense if they somehow connect to the common usage inherited from the past. Precisely because I do not have a perspicuous set of signs or symbols by which to make my experience of the personal visible to you, I must call upon the language and the history we share, pushing and pulling at the conventions of usage and sense in such a way as to alert you to the presence of the new. To do this, though, involves me in reflecting upon the received tradition, as I try to discern those complexes of events, ideas, words and images that are most serviceable for the task of contemporary communication. In making this selection I testify to my conviction that those whose words I now make my own had in their own time and place some analogue of the new that I am experiencing now. The possibility of such repetition across the unrepeatable difference marked by the passage of time lies at the root of the possibility of interpretation. Although I can never rescue the past from the ambiguity in which my own language is entrammelled, I can – and must – seek to interpret it as potentially revelatory of the novel and creatively personal depths of freedom that I believe myself to have experienced in the here and now. Only so can I come to an understanding of my own experience. Only so can I hope to make that experience intelligible to others.

All of this is a natural and, indeed, spontaneous impulse in the religious consciousness. We scarcely question the appropriateness of 'explaining' our faith by means of the great exemplars of piety and doctrine provided by the past. In teaching what the faith means we hold up the model lives of the saints and biblical heroes and heroines. Faith is what these people experienced and said and did. They are the mirrors in which our own faith becomes clear to us. This is true at the simplest Sunday School level and in the higher reaches of theological research. The study of the theology of the

Rhineland mystics or of Protestant scholasticism, of Kierkegaard or of the Oxford Movement, is never the purely objective, disinterested study of past facts (although it will always need to be attentive to the best available account of the facts). Such study is itself a part of the larger enterprise of interpreting the meaning of faith in its multiple refraction through the prism of history. And, of course, precisely because the testimony of history is itself ambiguous and its meaning cannot simply be read off the surface but requires interpretation, there is always the possibility of new readings (and, of course, new misreadings). What was once commended as a paradigmatic movement of the Spirit may be called into question as new evidence or new evaluative criteria become available. Most Western Christians would now be reluctant to extol the zeal of the Crusaders as matter for imitation, although the ideal of the Christian warrior is one that had considerable currency in the Christian world for many centuries. But new readings can be positive as well as negative. As a result of research made possible by feminist perspectives, outstanding women mystics, teachers and reformers have been rescued from oblivion, or from being dismissed as mad or hysterical. Even the ordinary and the unexciting, the unresearched and the minor, marginal figures can become the occasion or the focus of powerful, transformative reappraisals of the tradition.

Although it is perhaps inevitable that communities will always strive towards some kind of normative canon, a core-curriculum of exemplary texts, events and personalities, the sheer scope, variety and interpretability of historical experience makes it unlikely that, practically speaking, the canon can ever be closed. For the Christian churches, the canon of scripture is, of course, theoretically closed. In practice, however, the unique authority of scripture is continually being qualified by the dynamics of tradition. This is, famously, something that Protestant critics have always been quick to observe in relation to Catholic and Orthodox churches, arguing that developments like the cult of Mary of the veneration of images not only go beyond scripture but subvert it. For the strictest of

Lutheran and Calvinist theologies, there can be no addition to scripture that does not obscure or corrupt the message of scripture itself. And yet Lutheran and Calvinist communities themselves are not – and, in fact, cannot be – entirely resistant to the growth and influence of tradition. The dramatic story of Luther's discovery of the principle of justification by faith alone and other exemplary conversion stories come to constitute a kind of tradition in Protestant communities, a lens through which to read and interpret scripture. The Protestant is never, in fact, alone with scripture. It is never simply a matter of the man of the twenty-first century sitting down with the man of the first century and listening to what he says. Such abstraction from history just isn't possible. In reading scripture the Protestant, no less than the Catholic, is, however invisibly, directed to privileged texts and preferred readings. The community – and once again we can see a qualified justification for the claims of cultural-linguistic and narrative theologies – mediates the individual's approach to the text.

Luther's sermons and Calvin's commentaries may not in principle have the same authority for Protestants as the theology of Aquinas officially has for Roman Catholics, but in practice the difference is not so sharp. Protestantism too has its greater and lesser doctors of the church – as well, it should be said, as innumerable exemplary Christian personalities: missionaries, martyrs and livers of holy lives.[6]

A number of years ago, the broadcaster Malcolm Muggeridge produced a television series in which he singled out Augustine, Pascal, Blake, Kierkegaard, Tolstoy and Bonhoeffer as constituting what he called *A Third Testament* (this being the title he gave the

---

[6] This intrusion (as some might see it) of a traditional dimension into Protestantism is, very probably, one of the reasons why Protestantism has proved so fissiparous, with Protestant churches repeatedly splitting into ever smaller, ever purer sects. If tradition is, in principle, excluded in favour of *sola scriptura*, and if it soon becomes obvious that traditional elements are in fact creeping into the life of a newly reformed church, the stage is set for a new generation of reformers, eager and willing to reform the reformation.

series). I suggest that churches and individuals are, in fact, continually engaged in the production of such 'third testaments', bodies of theological, devotional, hagiographical and other writings, symbols and practices that mediate the individual's understanding of religious truth. Without them, the truths set forth in scripture would be abstract and uninterpretable. The historical gap between the closing of the canon and our own time is simply too great for us to appropriate the message of scripture in any meaningful way without such mediation. At the simplest level of all, we do not now speak the languages of scripture. The words of revelation require translation, and even the great translations of the Reformation period have themselves become inaccessible to many contemporary readers and require revision or replacement – and, as is well-known, every translation is an interpretation, involving innumerable detailed decisions as to which of several possible meanings is to be preferred. Down to the minutiae of vocabulary and syntax, the production of a new translation cannot but reveal the translator's own intellectual and spiritual horizons. But translation alone is never enough. The newly translated text still needs to be explained and expounded. Rote-learning of the words is merely a beginning. We do not learn the meaning of even the simplest passages of scripture by means of straightforward propositional exposition. What story could be better-known in our culture than that of the Good Samaritan – and yet, as taught in school assemblies and preached from a thousand pulpits, learning what it means involves imaginatively re-enacting the story in the context of contemporary social situations, and the tensions between Jews and Samaritans (and between the various castes within Judaism) on which the story depends have to be reinterpreted in the light of the tensions pulling at the fabric of our own society.

Now I am not saying that this distorts the text. On the contrary, it is essential if the text is to be appropriated, actualized, and applied. What I am saying is that even in such cases, the text only enters into our contemporary reality by means of interpretation. It is not just a matter of reading it in the new contexts in which we now live; it is a matter of reading it *into* these contexts. Of course, once we move beyond the world of parables and heroic narratives, things rapidly become infinitely more complex. The concepts and categories by which the first Christian communities sought to name and frame the meaning of Jesus' life, death and resurrection are no longer part of our cultural currency, at least, not outside the sub-culture of church life. Messiah, Son of God, Son of Man, Lord, Saviour and the other titles of Jesus, titles that reflect the cultural horizons of the early church in its various phases, mean whatever they mean to us on the basis of their association with Christian claims, rather than being ways of interpreting and explaining those claims. We can only understand these titles in the light of our own understanding of historical expectation, representative personality and moral authority, and it is always a matter of debate as to how far these understandings are inter-changeable. If I think of Jesus Christ as 'Superstar' (which, I guess very few people really do, but the example highlights the problem well), it is far from self-evident that this 'title' gives me any serious insight into the kind of self-understanding or community under-tanding expressed in titles such as 'Messiah' or 'Son of God'. And the further we go into the theological complexities of the text, the more problematic the work of interpretation becomes, the more strained the tension between our horizons and those of the first century gets.

Two horizons are, in fact, never enough. The third testament always comes between. Such third testaments offer pathways – themselves sometimes daunting and dangerous – between our time and the time of the community's founding events. Muggeridge's particular third testament will not, of course, suit everybody, and once we begin to consider the actual part played by such bodies of tradition, we inevitably confront the fact of pluralism. That the dynamics of tradition-formation run in the direction of pluralism has long been recognized. The thirty-fourth article of the Church of England's articles of religion puts it nicely: 'It is not necesary that Traditions and Ceremonies be in all places one, and utterly like; for at all times they have been divers, and may be changed according to the diversities of countries, times, and men's manners . . .' New times and new places pose new questions, generate new readings and produce new models of sanctity that, in their turn, become signposts for their successors.

Tradition against traditionalism

Tradition, then, means traditions, and it is somewhat ironic that those who are called 'traditionalists' in contemporary church life are very often those who seek to deny or to restrain the dynamic pluralism of tradition-formation. Their stance is often reminiscent of that of the heritage culture that has grown up in the last thirty years and that is so profoundly troubling for the future development of church architecture. For an integral part of the power of many ancient church buildings is precisely the fact that they have grown and developed over many centuries, being constantly rebuilt in layer upon layer of styles and incorporating all manner of curiosities and contingencies. Suddenly, however, it is deemed that whatever state the building had reached in 19— is to be its definitive state for evermore. Change is not actually stopped, but it is subject to a range of conditions that, if applied in the past, would have prevented many of our finest parish churches from becoming what they now are. So with the ecclesiastical and theological traditionalists – only in their case the defining moment is not some time in the recent past but something more remote. Whether it is the church order of Vatican I, the enthusiasm of early Methodism, the theology of the Reformers or the great social, aesthetic and theological synthesis of the Middle Ages, or something still more distant (the experience of the Desert Fathers and Mothers or the heroic witness of the church of the martyrs), some single moment or movement is detached from its context in the total develoment of Christian life and doctrine and used as a template by which to impose a unitary (and often arbitrary) order on the ferment of history. Obviously, the impulse towards tradional*ism* in this reductionist sense is connected with the same impulse that generates the proliferation of third testaments that contribute so richly to the variegated brocade of Christian history. Where it differs is in its exclusivity, its manner of privileging one time and place or one line of development over all others. In the case of cruder forms of fundamentalism, the absurdity of such gestures of exclusivity is all too apparent to all those with any historical sense who are not prepared to accept a virtually schizophrenic dualism between their religious faith and the rest of their lives. There are, however, more sophisticated versions of the same tendency that are the more seductive, the larger the range of their historical vision. However, even if one takes as large a perspective as, say, theology before Duns Scotus and the advent of nominalism (a way of defining the topic that some schools of modern theology seem to find attractive[7]), it is ultimately stultifying to rend the continuum of historical becoming in such a way as to exclude the possibility of important innovation. To say that we still have much to learn from the past is one thing, but to turn a particular interpretation of a particular phase of the past into the exclusive source of norms for contemporary thinking is, basically, idolatry. (And, like most idols, our favoured historical moments usually turn out to have feet of clay, and to stand on very dubious or at least contestable historical readings.)

For those who accept the Reformation as a key element in orientating their theological vision, it is necessary to affirm that the church can err. For mainstream Protestantism the great falling-away occurred subsequent to the period of the ecumenical councils, a view that, for Protestant theologians, justifies their claim to genuine Catholicity. Since Kierkegaard and Overbeck, the 'great betrayal' has been pushed further back into the past and the view has gained ground that the Constantinian settlement already marks

---

[7] And that recalls the Japanese aestheticist who asserted that before the fourteenth century men produced only beautiful objects.

the triumph of an essentially anti-Christian view of the world, in which Hellenistic philosophical and political goals and imperatives have obscured the original thrust of New Testament Christianity. More recently still, some theologians have discerned the symptoms of corruption in the New Testament itself, as the original freedom of the primitive church was overtaken by the patriarchal structures reflected in the Pastoral Epistles. Paradoxically, then, the gesture of asserting that the church was (with whatever minor deviations and qualifications) on the right lines up until 'time x' is – wherever we choose to draw the line – a quintessentially Protestant gesture. But, no matter when or where or how it crept in, once the possibility of error is admitted, the whole question of 'by what authority?' is immediately brought to the top of the agenda. By what authority, by what right, with what reason do we maintain that the other is in error and we are of the truth? If the authority is merely authority, merely the gesture by which authority asserts itself as authoritative, then all argument is at an end. However, in our contemporary situation, such a move would be like a single policeman attempting to hold back a rioting crowd. For authority that is no longer recognized is no longer authority: it is the fantasy world of intellectual self-abuse.

If, on the other hand, there is some good reason for holding to one party or one perspective rather than another, then we must be prepared to show what that reason is, to argue our case and, in a word, to enter into dialogue. We can only do that, however, on the condition that we acknowledge the possibility that the line between truth and error does not lie between one and another church, one and another period of history, one and another theology or one and another individual, but runs through the middle of all of these. Whatever good reason we have for holding our view, we have to concede that others may have at least some good reason for holding to their contrary view.

The Protestant challenge to the principle of authority, when it does not generate its own, almost inevitably arbitrary forms of authoritarianism, can thus lead quite easily to a large and generous embrace of critical, dialogical rationality. From the seventeenth to the nineteenth centuries, it came naturally to many Protestant writers to identify Protestantism as a religion of reason. The protest against Rome was widened from being an argument about narrowly theological issues, and became the promotion of an intellectual culture in which the values of free enquiry, religious tolerance and social liberty were held up against what was perceived as the authoritarianism and obscurantism of Roman Catholicism. Such an identification between Protestantism and reasonable Christianity seems less obvious this side of the evangelical revival and other modern movements within the Protestant Churches, nor do I wish uncritically to endorse the often strident voice of Protestant polemics; nonetheless, there was a certain logic in this development. For once it is conceded that the church can err, we have also to concede that what happened once can happen again. Even if we believe that the church lived through some period of original purity (whether it lasted thirty or three hundred or thirteen hundred years before it fell away from its primitive state), we must all the more hesitate before claiming that we, as the children of the broken, fragmented and fallen church, are going to achieve a clear, unclouded vision of the truth. Coming out from under the rubble, we must make our way in the haze of dust thrown up by the great collapse, orientating ourselves in a strange new world from which the familiar landmarks have been erased. Acceptance of the principle of criticism places upon us the obligation of self-criticism. We must each, continually, consider the possibility that we may be mistaken. Furthermore, such considerations are not just a matter of practising the virtue of humility; they are themselves a spur to the ever more precise testing and refinement of such truth as we believe ourselves to possess. As I have argued, the process of dialogue is in fact the keenest, most demanding and most all-encompassing means of such testing and refinement.

Is this relativism?

Does this then mean that we are cast adrift in a sea of relativism, in which meaning is dissolved into a continually expanding multiplicity of diverse discourses, an endless flux of intellectual becoming?

Certainly there are those who tell the story this way: first came the golden age of mediaeval Christendom in which personal faith, institutional religion and intellectual understanding were harmoniously united in an unitary world-view; next came the Reformation, in which individual faith tore itself away from the body of the church, rending the fabric of Christendom, and permitting reason to slip the leash of ecclesiastical tutelage; from here it was only a short step to the next phase, the Enlightenment, and the kind of unilateral declaration of independence on the part of Reason that very quickly led to the out-and-out relativism and nihilism of Nietzsche and his heirs. Nor do those who see things this way miss the point that the most radical currents of nineteenth-century anti-religious thought were the spawn of philosophers, such as Hegel, whose minds had been shaped by the culture of Enlightenment Protestant theology.

However, there are other versions of the same historical progression that see it through the lenses of very different values. There are those among us, of course, who regard the whole process as 'a good thing', exactly reversing the conclusions of Catholic or Anglo-Catholic apologists. For many such, Nietzschean nihilism is, indeed, the 'truth' of how things are: all moral and religious truth (at the very least: perhaps scientific truth too) *is* arbitrary and relative. Like it or not, this is the situation to which we have to accommodate ourselves. In fact, some Nietzschean postmodernists assure us, once we have got over mourning for the lost god of the past, we will be free to embrace without reserve the joyful wisdom of the new age, and throw ourselves whole-heartedly into the playful dance of a new, but ironic, Dionysos. We will be both knowing and naïve, and life will never have been so good!

Such views are not exclusively those of the anti-religious. Some Christian voices have been heard proclaiming something similar. Nor is this as surprising as it might at first seem. For religion has often been lived and experienced more as a mode of enthusiastic life-affirmation than as a primarily theoretical construct, and has been the domain of visionaries and free spirits no less than of theologians and hierarchs.

The view that is being proposed here is not, however, a relativism of this kind. In order to explain the difference between my own position and those of the Neo-Medievalists and the Neo-Nietzscheans, I shall draw upon the distinction between the viewpoint of a spectator and that of a participant, a distinction which is by no means original but which I nonetheless find valuable.

That the task of theoretical reflection is to give us a picture of how things look from the viewpoint of a spectator is implicit in the very concept of theory. In some philosophies, perhaps those of Plato and of Hegel, the aim of getting an unobscured view of truth or of the totality of the world process seems to be regarded as achievable in principle. In the theatre of history the philosopher finds himself installed in the very best seat. Since the early nineteenth century, however, the idea that there is any one position from which it is possible to see the whole picture has fallen into disrepute. Wherever we place ourselves, our vision will be foreshortened, distorted or interrupted in one way or another. The result is that we must make do with a sequence of limited, provisional 'takes', snapshots and 'stills' of a vast moving spectacle that overflows all possibilities of definitive representation. One way of conceptualizing this situation is Nietzsche's perspectivism, that is, the belief that there are only points of view and no single, all-encompassing panorama. Herman Hesse's novel *Steppenwolf* was to provide a marvellous exploration of this idea in the image of the 'magic theatre', where each box looks out on to a novel and unrepeatable drama: all is play, make-believe, and the highest wisdom is not to take any of it too seriously. 'Reality' is held at bay by the kaleidoscopic variety of images with which the eye of the spectator is dazzled and kept entertained.[8]

Over against the spectator stands the participant: believer, activist, *engagé*. Whether in the manner of the medieval believer who spontaneously lives and breathes the atmosphere of the given religious culture, or the twentieth-century existentialist who achieves participation by personal decision and active ethical or political involvement, the participant has an immediate rapport with reality (and even with Being) that the mere spectator can never achieve. Compared with the spectator, the participant may be inarticulate and unrefined, but this weakness in respect of theory is more than compensated for by the compensatory strength and vigour of 'real life'.

How does this relate to the confrontation between the Neo-Medievalist and the Neo-Nietzschean?

The Neo-Medievalist typically holds that the circle can be squared and that vision is possible on the basis of participation. One can both hold to a particular faith (*this* faith, the tradition of the church) and experience the whole. Everything has its place within the hierarchy of Being. The Neo-Nietzschean, as we have seen, believes that participation excludes any kind of holistic vision and that, as participants in the flow and torrent of life, we can see no more than a succession of more or less rapidly moving images, pictures and interpretations that orientate us in the flux of

---

[8] Such an image seems particularly apposite in the case of the modern city-dweller, who is subject to a level of rapidly-changing visual stimuli that is unprecedented in history, culminating in the concept of virtual reality: what 'is' is indistinguishable from what 'seems' to be. Philosophy, having begun amongst the city-dwellers of Athens, whose (free) citizens could not only be gathered into the space of a single auditorium but who could believe themselves to be defined by a single, unifying vision/theory, meets its nemesis in the megalopolitan culture of the late twentieth century, in which the sheer scale of the modern city overruns all conceivability, and one image flashes past the next with ungraspable speed. The line between reality and virtual reality begins to blur and 'home' is only an imagined memory.

becoming, but that have no intrinsic purchase on Being, on what, in any serious sense, is 'really real'.

I claimed in Chapter 1 that the kind of view I am attributing here to the Neo-Medievalist is not in fact credible in the contemporary world. The destiny of knowledge in our time is such that there can be no single science of Being and no unambiguous experience of Being. But does it follow that we are handed over, 'without reserve', to relativism?

The relativist, as described here, is a curious mix of spectator and participant. His relativism is largely conditioned by the fate that, as participant, he thereby denies himself the metaphysical elevation that would enable him to see the whole. Struggling in the swell and surge of existence – anxiously or joyously as the case may be! – he cannot attain the serene heights of Platonic contemplation. Yet he does not forswear the pleasures of spectatorship entirely. Although he has abandoned all ambitions regarding the whole picture, he does believe himself to have a pretty good view of the past. If the present and the future remain shrouded in uncertainty, the past has, as it were, fossilized into representability. What was once open, uncertain and at risk has become fixed, certain and settled. The Nietzschean knows that, however little he 'knows' in the classical sense of the word, he 'knows' a great deal more than his forebears knew. He can see them in a way they could never see themselves. He has arrived at a point in history from which he can look back and down at them: they have become pure 'outside', transparent to his gaze. He can read their motives, understand their intentions, and think their thoughts better than they could themselves. As he now sees it, the successive forms of consciousness through which humanity has passed have become exhaustively decipherable in the light of the present. He knows that he cannot exist, cannot live, cannot *be*, as those in the past existed, lived and, once, were. The past no longer *is*, it is just a memory. The forms of life that were once filled by those who lived in and through them have become empty forms, mere illustrations in the story I now tell about myself. I know the past, not as the traditionalist believes he knows it – as a repository of ontological fullness –, but simply as the narration of my own genealogy. The ladder that helped me to ascend to the heights of the present can be pushed away once its work is done and I am safely installed in the here and now. Metaphysics is dissolved into history, but the relativist takes up a role of spectatorship in relation to this history that his gaze penetrates and dominates as confidently as that of any metaphysician ever did.

That the solidity of the past can thus evaporate into the ether-like medium of representation, where it is looked at but not lived in, is an assumption that is integral to the relativist's project. Emancipation from the past and participation in the present are interconnected in such a way that the transformation of the actuality of the past into mere representation is one of the principal means by which the Nietzschean relativist is able to legitimate his celebration of the present at the expense of the past. The past no longer touches him in the centre of his conscious existence, and so it appears to him that all views deriving from the past, all traditions, creeds and institutions, are equally valid and equally empty.

But what if the relativist was mistaken? What if our identity is in fact inseparable from the past? Not, as I have already suggested, in the sense that we are prisoners of the past, mere effects of past causes, helpless links in a deterministic chain of causation, but rather in the sense that who we are now is interdependent with our history? It is not, as it is for the relativist, that the past is the mere prelude or lead-in to the present; it is rather that the past lives on or lives again in the present, as I take up the questions, challenges and situations bequeathed me by the past and make them the matter of my present efforts at self-understanding and self-improvement. In terms of the dialectic of participation and spectatorship, I still participate too deeply and too extensively in the past (and it in me) for me ever to achieve the kind of distance or detachment that would be necessary for me to become a spectator of my own history. No matter how distant the time of which we are speaking, the essential unfinishedness of history means that I cannot lay down in advance the limits as to when, where or how the past may, sometimes quite suddenly, become vitally and transformatively, creatively or destructively, a power in the present.[9]

In the process of dialogue by which I come to be who I am, the past is a dynamic and formative factor. Previously, I used the image of fossilization to describe how the relativist sees the past, as a succession of types, each having its own small place in the museum of history. But it would be a mistake to think of even a fossil as having arrived at a fixed and final state. The geological cycle is not finished when a life-form is thus turned to stone. We may tear the fossil from the ground, examine it in our laboratories and display it in our museums *as if* it has reached some sort of definitive finality, but that is already to risk a kind of intellectual petrification more rigid than that of the earth's own way of dealing with its products. In reality each stratum of the earth's surface continues to be subject to pressure and counter-pressure. Stability itself is only ever relative, but it is precisely this chronic instability and openness to change that makes it impossible for me to adapt the spectatorial pose of the relativist for whom the past has become a mere gallery of ideas, images and laws. The past continues to participate in the present, and I, in this very present, participate in the past. Self-interpretation and the understanding of history (personal, collective and natural) are indissolubly interconnected.

The course of my argument at this point may seem to be pointing

---

[9] It is striking how the historical and archaeological study of even the most ancient peoples continues to provide the focus for burning political arguments, as contemporary claims relating to nationhood and territory seek legitimacy by viewing themselves in the distant mirror of the remote past. Striking contemporary examples include the study of the early urban civilizations of Mesopotamia, the Scythians of the lands to the north of the Black Sea, or the inhabitants of pre-Columbian America, or, perhaps most contentiously of all, the peoples of ancient Palestine. That many of these claims appear to the liberal Western reader to be self-evidently pseudo-historical does not, however, entirely explain away the impulse behind such examples, namely, the sense that who we are now is profoundly and importantly influenced by our history and that the past lives on or lives again in our contemporary problems and opportunities.

towards the kind of existentialist position associated with existentialist theologians such as Bultmann. Certainly, Bultmann's theology was led by questions not dissimilar to those that concern us here, but the manner of addressing them was very different. Nor is this difference to do with the fact that I am allowing a much larger and broader role for tradition than Bultmann, with his Lutheran emphasis on *sola scriptura*, ever could. If tradition is vindicated simply as a means of providing a context for my contemporary existential concerns, if tradition is merely the occasion for me to formulate an understanding of the God-relationship by which I am gripped in the present, then I will stand accused, with Bultmann, of reducing the past (in his case scripture, in mine tradition) to being a mere cipher of the present. My only solution to relativism, it will be said, is the arbitrary assertion by the presently-existing self of its own passions and commitments, 'mere subjectivism'. However – and this is where the position for which I am arguing differs in formulation from that of Bultmannian existentialism –, it is essential to hold in mind that precisely because the self is not envisaged here as a completely individuated entity, but as coming to be what it is in and through dialogue, in and through the encounter with the other, its personal and historical self-understanding will never be purely arbitrary or subjective. From the ground up, in its deepest roots and most elaborate branchings, the self-understanding at which I arrive will be tested in dialogue, and this dialogue will, in at least some of its aspects, involve confronting the challenge of critical rationality. Repeatedly I must honour the obligation of accountability, because the understanding at which I have arrived is never 'my own' in an absolute sense, although it only becomes 'my' understanding as and to the extent that I assume responsibility for it.[10]

---

[10] These comments should indicate why I believe that my position has a built-in check against the kind of appropriation of history that uncritically hijacks particular interpretations of the past in the cause of contemporary ideologies of class, nation, state or grouping of states. Fascistic and other extreme nationalist historiography provides plentiful examples of this kind of thing.

The past, then, lives on in the formative traditions in which we participate, and which provide the impetus and the direction of our thinking and which, thereby, become available as a context in which to express and articulate the novum that is the gift of the present.

From the shock of the new to future shock

But what of the future?

Even if I have succeeded in showing how a dynamic and open understanding of tradition can liberate us from the sclerosis of traditionalism and allow for the spontaneous impulse of the past to make itself present in an expansive and enriching manner, the picture I have drawn may seem to be excessively backward-looking. Here I am, experiencing in my present the irruption of the *novum*, the transformative, creative novelty of divine love; seeking to interpret this experience to others, I turn to the past, to the words, images and rituals of the tradition, as providing a language in which to make public what must otherwise remain hidden in the inner depths of religious feeling. But is the construction of meaning in which I am engaged confined to a line that runs to and fro between present and past? Does it not, must it not, also involve the future?

Now although the future is, notoriously, worryingly (and, perhaps, obviously) unknowable in a far more radical sense than the past, it would seem odd to regard the future as being qualitatively different from past and present. For we know that the present is what it is only as a constant movement from the past into the future: the future is just what emerges from the present (and, therefore, from the past). The present will become future and the future will become past. Long ago, Ecclesiastes predicted that what will be is only what has been, and what has been is what will recur many times, until the world's end, and even if we do not want to go as far as endorsing the cyclical view of time implied in these words, we may take them as indicative of a kind of continuity running through the whole range of our time-experience.

Certainly, the present participates in the future no less than it does in the past. Experiencing the *novum* of love is not some pure encounter in which my sense of presence has absorbed all of time into an eternal now. Because this experience involves understanding myself as accountable to the other, it has a moral dimension, an orientation towards mutual action and the mutual transformation of self and other that is intrinsically futural. The question 'Who am I?' is indissociable from the question 'What, then, shall I *do*?'. Theoretical self-understanding and practical self-direction are reciprocally conditioning. If truth is not identical with goodness, the pursuit of truth and the pursuit of goodness are inextricably intertwined. The strongest arguments for metaphysics have been those that look to metaphysics as a guide to morals, i.e., that metaphysics exist *for the sake of* morals. And morals, as involving action, are essentially future-directed. Morality is not just a matter of our sitting in judgment on world-history or of drawing up abstract codes of moral rules, but of directing ourselves (dialogically) towards the tasks that still need to be done, the duties and obligations that remain, as yet, unfulfilled, incomplete, crying out for action.[11]

Concern for the future, then, is no less central to the unfolding of the dialogical process than the interpretation of the past. But concern for the future takes many forms, and we shall need to be no less critical of some of these forms than we have been of traditionalism. Indeed, one of the most striking manifestations of humanity's concern for the future is the perennial phenomenon of utopianism. Whereas some find their golden age in the past, others are no less drawn towards some imagined future state. However, although the spirit of utopia may at first glance seem more hospitable towards the spirit of radical novelty, exactly the same objections can be made to utopianism as to traditionalism. In each case a particular moment is singled out of the total historical process and used as a criterion by which to evaluate the whole. In the case of utopianism, moreover, this is done on the basis of a

---

[11] For a further discussion of the ethical character of the dialogism I am proposing see Chapter 5 below.

purely imagined state of affairs, a state of affairs that has never been and may never be. Although the traditionalist's view of the past is typically so rose-coloured as to give a false tint to every aspect of his ideal world, there is at least some evidence available to argue the case for and against his version of history. In the case of the utopist, even this evidence is unavailable. Both the postulate of utopia and the critique of utopia operate within the aether of imagination – a reason, perhaps, why some of the most powerful critiques of utopianism have been in the form of novels, George Orwell's *1984* and *Animal Farm*, Aldous Huxley's *Brave New World* and *Island*, Yevgenny Zamyatin's *We* and Ray Bradbury's *Fahrenheit 451*.[12]

Against utopianism it has to be said that just as there is no golden age in the past, so there is no golden age in the future, no millennial messianic kingdom, no perfect society. At the level of chronological time, history may quite possibly come to an end in the sense that the universe will cease to be capable of supporting self-conscious life-forms; on the other hand, we have no reason to suppose that it will come to an end in the sense of arriving at a final destination, a moment (or even an everlasting kingdom) of completion or fulfilment. Our lives, then, cannot be justified by what their historical results will be, any more than history as a whole can be justified by its results. The view that the verdict of history constitutes the Last Judgment is a view that will always lead to depression if not to despair. For history yields no more than provisional 'results', results the meaning of which depends on interpretative processes that are themselves unfinished. The 'end' of history in the qualitative sense can never be presumed to coincide with any past or present state of affairs, any result or set of results that we can conceive of as issuing forth from the historical

---

[12] The conceptual analogies between traditionalism and utopianism facilitate a curious sub-genre of utopistic writing, in which the perfect civilization of the future is portrayed as the rediscovery of a lost civilization of the past. From Bacon onwards, Atlantis has been a favoured figure of such 'lost' but 'higher' civilizations.

process. If history is to be justified, it is as the matrix and the milieu from within which meaning, freedom and personality emerge. As that emergence has been described in these pages it is something that is always experienced as a *novum*, inexplicable in terms of what has come before and what will come after, and irreducible to any kind of historical causation. At the same time, as I have also insisted, the meaning of this *novum* can only be expressed and understood in terms of the communicative resources bequeathed us by tradition, although, as we are now seeing, the past – tradition – cannot itself be isolated from the present and the future. As a bearer and interpreter of tradition, I am simultaneously engaged by present concerns that are, in turn, conditioned by my bearing towards what is still to come. It is just this mutual interrogation of past, present and future that prevents tradition from congealing into traditionalism, the new from being trivialized as the trendy and the future from transforming itself into an unachievable utopia.

But if, as I have claimed, the historical process 'justifies' itself in terms of the emergence within it of the radical novelty of freely creative persons, interpreted in and through the dynamics of dialogue, we are confronted by one further, burning question.

For, it will be objected, I have too easily let slip the idea of a temporal goal of history: isn't the Judaeo-Christian tradition fundamentally committed to the view that, no matter how many dangers, toils and snares it has to negotiate on the way, history will arrive at the New Jerusalem, the kingdom of the Messiah, the rule of God? History, in the biblical perspective, is not without aim or purpose. It begins in time and it ends in time, and everything that happens in between is determined by what will be revealed at that end-time. Nor is the motivation lying behind such claims simply a matter of apocalyptic curiosity. It is, in its roots, passionately moral. For whatever lessons history may or may not have to teach us, one thing does seem fairly certain on the basis of our historical experience so far: that countless individuals, men, women and children (not to mention animals and other life forms), have perished in circumstances of utter and overwhelming misery;

millions have endured lives in which their value as persons has been unable to achieve expression: abused, insulted, injured and disfigured, the victims of Auschwitz, Hiroshima, the Somme and more human and natural tragedies than our chronicles have recorded have been swallowed up in a fog of hideous and unrelieved meaninglessness and hurt. What can history mean to them? If we say that history has no final goal, that there is no purpose, no great End, to it all, are we not condemning such victims to a second death, creating a tragic universe in which, perhaps, the ungodly do triumph and might is right? The version of dialogism I have put forward here would seem to be reduced to silence in the face of such questions. At best it might be capable of promoting a kind of stoicism in which we collectively keep our spirits up by going on talking as we journey deeper and further into the cosmic night, but which falls far short of vital, enlivening hope.

Certainly, I have committed myself to accepting that the principle of dialogue cannot leap over the barriers of history and endorse an eschatological vision that proclaims 'All shall be well!' on the plane of chronological time. Dialogue cannot achieve what no other theology or metaphysic has, in fact, ever achieved: provision of a conclusive, objective case for believing that, in the final end of all things, wrongs will be righted and the innocent victims compensated with everlasting bliss. We can only see in a glass, darkly. Nonetheless, however enigmatic, hope remains the mirror in which we best see the past.

Thus, just as dialogical interpretation may, and perhaps must, avail itself of the resources of tradition if it is to make personal experience a matter of public discourse, so too it may, and perhaps must, draw upon the common discourse about the future if it is to do full justice to the experienced *novum* of personality (since, as I have argued, the future, no less than the past, participates actively in all present experience). As a way of articulating its sense of the personal – the height, depth, length and breadth of all that is implied by that word – radical dialogism may justifiably appropriate the eschatological symbols of the religious traditions. Indeed, it is likely that it will have recourse to these symbols just as spontaneously as it has recourse to the exemplary forms and figures of the past. Job's declaration 'I know that my redeemer liveth!' epitomizes this spontaneous passion of personality in the face of meaningless and utter extinction: the conviction that the innocent will not be forgotten for ever. Nor is Job speaking for himself alone in this great cry from the depths; because the justice he seeks is the justice of God the creator, it embraces all victims. If I say 'I know that my redeemer liveth', I commit myself to believing that the redeemer lives for others no less than for me. The pursuit of a future in which God can enter into the polyphony of human voices is not a private passion, but arises out of a concern for common transformation that can only be explained and realized by the process of dialogue.

The unfolding of the content of dialogical life in terms of time, then, is a matter both of retrieved memory and committed hope. In the labour of weaving together the dimensions of past and future, a labour that is the ever-present challenge of dialogism, the meaning that the other has for and through me and that I have for and through the other begins to acquire concreteness. *What* I believe to be revealed in the dialogical situation is the belief of *this* tradition and the hope of *this* future. The conditions of historical life are such that my striving to find and to express personal meaning and personal value will always have a quite specific form. I cannot create my own religious universe in a vacuum, but must work with the conditions, limitations and opportunities that flow from the fact that I live in time. But because 'what' I believe and hope is generated by the dialogical encounter, it is constantly obliged to return to its roots and to submit itself to scrutiny by those others amongst whom my life is set. I cannot and should not hope to shirk this discipline, which will, in our present circumstances, often take the form of a rational interrogation as to the reasons, grounds and consequences of my belief and hope, although, equally, it may take the form of mutual affirmation or the opening of hitherto undreamed of horizons of understanding and imagination. In any case, it is virtually certain that, whilst the commitment to dialogue will yield both an extensive and an intensive respect for and engagement with tradition, and require us to frame some vision of things to come, it will at the same time prove to be the most powerful antidote to all traditionalisms and utopianisms.

4

The Contexts of Thinking about God

Theology and thinking about God in church and academy

We have become used to thinking that ideas are inseparable from history and that both the form and content of thought vary from age to age. The religious culture of the late Middle Ages faced different questions and challenges from those confronting the early eighteenth century, which, in turn, are different from those we face today. Even when theology insists that its essential truths remain unchanged, from age to age the same, it is accepted that the expression of those truths must adapt to changing historical circumstances. Even the theology of twenty years ago looks and feels very different from the theology of today. As I have argued in the preceding chapter, however, the dynamics of change do not just affect the outward expression of religion, they penetrate its very core. Thinking about God is born in a dialogical process that is historical through and through.

Such reflections no longer surprise us. We are, however, less used to thinking about the role played by the spatial or institutional location of thinking about God. Liberation theology has, to be sure, warned that it is one thing to theologize in the ivory towers of a Western academic institution and something else again to theologize alongside the poor in their struggle for basic human rights. But although thinking about God within the Christian tradition will at some point require facing up to global issues of social justice, there are important differences amongst the privileged theoretical discourses that have to do with the different ways in which these discourses are institutionalized within Western society itself. Although the great divide between rich and poor can never be overlooked, and will (rightly) nag at the consciences of those who think about God within the security of the Western economic fold, there are increasingly important divisions between the kind of thinking about God that takes place in the context of public universities and the kind of thinking about God that takes place within the church, even within the confines of a particular society or of a homogenous social group. These divisions will be the focus of the first part of this chapter.

But if the academy and the church constitute distinctive sites whose institutional identities profoundly affect the way in which the task of thinking about God is undertaken within them, neither of them exists in isolation. The North American Catholic theologian David Tracy added to the list a further site of theological reflection, namely, 'society', arguing that neither church nor academy can ever completely separate themselves from the kind of religious questioning and practice found in the wider society of which they are each a part. I shall, therefore, follow Tracy by attempting to sketch how I see this larger social context interacting with the distinctive ways of thinking about God found in church and academy. But it doesn't stop there. For although mainstream theology has spent a generation freeing itself from what is perceived as the extreme individualism of religious existentialism, I wish to argue that thinking about God is never going to be exhausted by the public discourses of church, academy and society. Thinking about God would not matter to any of us if it did not reach into our ineluctably individualized struggles to live good lives in the face of moral failings and mortal weaknesses. I shall, then, conclude by adding a fourth site of thinking about God to Tracy's threesome of church, academy and society: the individual. Nor, I shall argue, does this undermine the principle of dialogue that I have claimed to be an essential characteristic of non-ontological thinking about God. For the individual does not need to be absolutized into some sort of metaphysical principle of subjectivity (as perhaps happened in some forms of German idealism). Rather, the individual is conceived of here precisely as one whose self-assertion and self-discovery is inseparable from the exigency of dialogue – but more of that later: let us now return to the question as to how the various contexts of church and academy affect the manner and meaning of thinking about God.

Some of the differences between theology in the church and theology in the academy are obvious to the point of banality. Whereas a parish church might advertise courses on 'How to Pray' or a church-based training scheme offer a module on 'The Arts in Gospel Perspective', a university-based theologian would be more likely to be addressing questions like 'The *Concept* of Prayer' or 'Foundations of Theological Aesthetics'. The church environment has, naturally and properly, been orientated towards practice, and the academy towards theory and history. On the other hand, this kind of difference meant something else within the era of ontology from what it means today. For it belonged to the assumptions of that era that practice and theory, history and metaphysics, shared a common and assured foundation. The practice was a putting into practice of the theory and the theory a theorization of the practice. The parish priest and the theologian were fellow-workers within a common enterprise. Indeed, it was possible for an individual to migrate between the two roles without undue difficulty.

Today, however, church and academy can no longer make the assumption of common ground. This has next to nothing to do with some supposed *trahison des clercs*, but a lot to do with the fact that, within the context of the academy, theologians can no longer *assume* that the claims of faith are accepted or even respected by fellow academicians.

It does not immediately follow that theology has *no* place in the modern university, although it does mean that its place will have to be defined and justified in quite other terms than those of metaphysical guardianship. Briefly, theology will be tolerated in the modern university on the same basis and within the same constraints as any other humanistic discipline. But is it possible for theology so to redefine itself without defining itself out of existence? What, in other words, is theology so redefined but religious studies, i.e. the study of the human history, understanding and phenomenology of religion? But is that *theo*-logy in any significant sense? Is it a thinking whose orientation, methodology and results are determined as thinking about God? Of course, God and the gods will be frequently mentioned in the pursuit of religious studies, but this does not mean that they are the true subject-matter of such studies. Nor does the fact that many people will be led to religious studies by their personal religious quest or conviction mean that their scholarship thereby becomes the self-understanding of faith, even if it gains a certain existential flavouring.

Some may dismiss these comments as an over-reaction, and, indeed, an over-reaction that is easily dealt with by looking at the facts. For, it will be said, the fact is that theology – and often quite specifically Christian theology – does survive as a university subject in many of the mainstream universities of the Western world. Indeed, Cambridge, where I am sitting and writing this book, boasts a faculty that embraces both theology and religious studies, and the former is by no means downgraded or displaced by the presence of the latter. Many students simultaneously study papers in theology *and* in religious studies without, for the most part, noticing any radical differences in terms of method or metaphysical assumptions.

It is almost unavoidable that, wherever we are, we regard the situations with which we are most familiar as representing the norm. However, once we start to look beyond our own immediate locale, it is striking how differently these things are managed in the various countries of the Western world. Compare, for example, the situation in Germany and Scandinavia with that in Great Britain, and compare that again with the United States. In each case we have a quite distinct model reflecting quite distinct historical developments and cultural attitudes. Reflecting on these different

models and practices will, I believe, help us to return, with greater
clarity, to the question how it is possible to go on thinking about
God and what form such thinking might take in our time.

Although Germany and the Scandinavian nations are widely
regarded as amongst the world's most secularized and tolerant
societies, it is, perhaps surprisingly, still the case that religion is
integrated into the state in a manner and to a degree unknown in
Britain and America. Established religion is supported through the
tax system and clergy are paid and employed on the same basis as
schoolteachers or civil servants. Moreover, we find the curious
situation that, whereas Scandinavia is exclusively Lutheran, Germany gives equal footing to Catholicism and Protestantism, each
commanding more or less equal support amongst the population
and each, correspondingly, receiving the equivalent financial
support from the state.

One aspect of this situation is that theology, as taught and
studied at university level, is not only a part of the general academic
life of the university, but also serves to promote the confessional
interests of the respective churches and to provide one of the
primary contexts of clergy training. In Germany this means that
there are both Catholic and Protestant faculties operating in the
university system, often in the same universities, and owing
allegiance to the church as much as to the university. Thus, when
the Catholic authorities withdrew Hans Küng's accreditation as a
teacher of the Catholic faith, he was no longer able to hold office in
the Catholic faculty of Tübingen University. In this case the
University solved the problem by inventing a new post outside
the faculty for him, although it is perhaps questionable whether
such a solution might have been available for someone of less
distinction.[1] The case does, however, highlight the oddity (human-
ists would say the scandal) of the situation that, in a society whose

---

[1] However, the reader should not conclude that I regard this as an
exclusively Catholic problem. Analogous, though less publicized cases have
arisen in the context of Protestant theology.

ethos is largely secular, whose government is democratic and in which there is no formal role for religious organizations in the legislature (unlike that played in Britain by Anglican bishops in the British House of Lords or by the sovereign as head of the established church), the state appears directly to endorse the beliefs of a specific faith community. It is doubly curious in the German context, where the state simultaneously supports and endorses the beliefs of two distinct faith communities, when, in many particular points, these two communities are marked by profound and as yet unresolved differences. Nor is this endorsement simply extrinsic, as would be the case if it was merely a matter of, say, leasing publicly-owned buildings to one or other church or to members of other faith communities living in Germany. Because we are talking about public universities, we are talking about institutions whose *raison d'être* is the pursuit of truth. Logic would suggest that the state thus finds itself in the position of simultaneously endorsing two distinct systems of truth.

Of course, it could be objected that this is simply a special case of the frequently observed phenomenon of an academic subject finding itself divided between two or more mutually rivalrous camps, a phenomenon no less well known in science than in such fields as literature, history or sociology. In some cases academics can scarcely agree amongst themselves as to what the discipline is about. But there is a difference, and it is this. In all other disciplines, these divisions are (supposedly!) internal to the subject itself and can, in principle, if not in fact, be fully and appropriately addressed within the academy, by means of normal academic methods. In most academic subjects there is a tacitly agreed space of acceptable controversy and dissent, and even when the dispute is not so much as to who has the right answers but as to the fundamental nature of the questions and methods of enquiry, there are ways and means of determining what counts as good or appropriate forms of argument. In the case of theology, however, it seems to be permissible to allow arguments and assertions to hold sway that the academy is not regarded as competent to judge. The academic standing of a teacher of theology is of no avail if he crosses a line drawn by the church.

Obviously the case of Hans Küng is an extreme; it is not unique, but it is certainly rare. Like many systems that seem to be inconsistent when subjected to logical scrutiny, the bipartisan structures of theology in German universities seem, for the most part, to work in practice thanks, doubtless, to the prudence, tact and intelligence of many of those who run it.

But consider how bizarre the whole system seems when viewed from the perspective of the United States. Here, reflecting the separation of church and state built into the American Constitution, 'theology' has today become almost exclusively the province of the seminary, i.e. the private, church-based, confessional and vocationally-oriented institution of higher education, whilst a public university or college will confine itself to 'religion' or 'religious studies'. Any whisper that a department of religion is giving special privileges to any particular faith community will arouse instant scandal (and possibly litigation), just as it would if were handing out or withholding privileges on the grounds of race, sexual preference or gender. It is easy for the European to dismiss this in terms of the excesses of political correctness, but its roots lie deep in the psyche and polity of America.

Here, as elsewhere, Britain finds itself in a muddled middle ground between the two systems. Although the Church of England and the Church of Scotland have a certain role within the political establishment of their respective nations, this role does not map on to the academic system in the same way as in Germany and Scandinavia. Although, in England, higher education only became available for non-Anglicans in the nineteenth century, and although the Church of England retains a number of varied vested interests in many institutions of higher education, there is no faculty of theology within the state system teaching exclusively Anglican theology. Perhaps in the 1950s it might well have been the case that some faculties were, in practice, thoroughly Anglican in ethos, but despite that dominance being taken for granted, it was only patchily built in to the constitution of academic theology. If, more loosely, a certain 'churchiness' or a vague Christian orientation is still tolerated, and often assumed, in British universities, this is not of the confessional kind found in northern Europe, although, from an American perspective, it looks uncomfortably biassed against minority points of view.

So is it the case that the northern European model represents that of the old world and that of America the new, and is the old fated to give way to the new, however long the process might prove? Will Britain first and Europe later follow America's secular lead, with clear blue water emerging between the religiously neutral academic discipline of religious studies and the church-based discipline of theology? And, if so, what are the consequences for thinking about God – whether in the university or in the church?

There is no doubt that there are many in Britain and Europe who regard the existence of theology as a university subject as a survival of an earlier age, tenaciously clinging on to an ever-diminishing field and destined soon to be supplanted by its young rival, religious studies. Indeed, that might seem to be the practical outcome of the crisis of metaphysics outlined in the opening chapter.

The prognosis is plausible – and yet there are a number of factors that might make us hesitate before signing up to it.

For one, this view ignores, or does not take sufficiently seriously, the presence of liberal values in faith communities themselves, and the different ways in which such communities may themselves have internally-generated reasons for defending and promoting the pluralism of public religious discourse.

Examples are readily available. Thus, it is in America, not Europe, that, for all the separation of powers, public schools are coming under pressure (and, in some cases, succumbing to pressure) from evangelical fundamentalism to tone down the teaching of evolutionary science. Conversely, the churches of West Germany (as it was then) played a leading role in the anti-nuclear movement of the early 1980s, at a time when the most politically dominant religious voice in America was that of the moral majority, and when non-established but politically aggressive religious groups gave ideological aid and comfort to Pentagon hawks by suggesting that an all-out nuclear war might just be the awaited fulfilment of biblical prophecy. The problem that these contrasts highlight is that in a situation where the state declines *in principle* to privilege any one religious group over any other it can easily be the case that the most socially influential forms of religion end up being those that are best able to harness nationalistic, populist and other social currents that are often profoundly anti-liberal. By a corresponding logic, the churches that are most established, far from being the most oppressive (which was perhaps true in the era of absolutism), are, in practice, often the most open to social change, being structurally committed to a continuing dialogue with the changing society around them.[2]

We might therefore hesitate before insisting too forcefully on the claim that religious establishment contradicts the principles of a liberal and open society. We might, on the contrary, do better to see such establishment as constitutive of one of a number of civic institutions that, by mediating between the state, the local community and the individual, maintain a diverse social environment and help to secure the concrete possibilities of free citizenship. It is minimally worth reflecting that the Scandinavian countries have achieved one of the most libertarian political cultures in the world whilst maintaining a model of religious establishment that, in America, would be denounced by all liberal-minded, constitution-loving citizens as quasi-fascistic, were anyone ever to attempt to impose such a model there.

---

[2] This is, of course, the reason why some believers regard the established churches as hopelessly compromised with the world. Kierkegaard's attack on the Danish establishment, and Newman's conversion to Roman Catholicism, were two striking examples of nineteenth-century religious figures who sought to opt out of the church's historic compromise with modernity; and the complaint that the established churches are too liberal, too eager to follow the agenda of the world, is one of the recurrent motifs of contemporary religious controversy.

I should stress that I really am saying no more than I am saying. My argument is not a circuitous subterfuge to defend the present *status quo* as regards the Anglican establishment in England. All I am saying is that there is no simple, unequivocal or universal correlation between the secularization of public institutions and the preservation of actual political and religious liberty.

I have another point, and it is this: that, whether or not a particular society has an established religion, there are a variety of ways in which the state can endorse and meet half-way the aspirations of religious communities to play as full a part as they can in the public life of their society.

A particular example that illustrates this point well is the existence of religious schools within the state school system in the United Kingdom. As so often, history has produced an intellectually anomalous but more or less practicable situation. The role of, principally, the Church of England in pioneering free education meant that, at the time when the state educational system was systematized (1944), the Church was able to insist on a special status for church schools, allowing the teaching of confessionally specific beliefs and the use of religious criteria in the selection of staff and appointment of governors. How this actually works out in practice has varied enormously. In some cases the local school is virtually an extension of the parish church, in others the church presence has dwindled to vanishing point. Until recently, these arrangements were limited to Anglican, Catholic, Methodist and Jewish schools. Permission has now been given for a Muslim school to be incorporated into the maintained sector on the same basis. This move has proved controversial in many quarters, not least because of the widespread perception in British society that Islam is virtually coterminous with what is called fundamentalist Islam. However, natural justice would seem to require that, if there are to be religious schools maintained by the state, non-Christian faith communities should be acceptable if they meet the same criteria as Christian schools. This leads to the more positive point that, precisely because such schools can only be given aided or controlled status if they are able to meet the same academic and other standards required of all public schools, they provide a way of engaging the energies of faith communities for public education. Although the fear is expressed in some quarters that by admitting such schools the state is, in effect, subsidizing alien growths within the body politic, the opposite view is at least worth some consideration. This view starts from the observation that, far from being a sign that the Muslim community is seeking to withdraw into an ideological ghetto, the active campaigning by Muslims for Islamic schools within the state system is a sign of their eagerness to play a full and proper role in the pluralistic society of modern Britain and of their desire to integrate the education of their children into the public sphere and their willingness to permit that education to be scrutinized by the state.

Of course, like all political arrangements, this is something that could go spectacularly wrong in a number of ways. Many would want to argue that the role of confessionally divided education in Northern Ireland has been to perpetuate the fears and divisions that characterize that region, and that have provided the atmosphere in which bloody mayhem has wrecked the lives of many thousands of people. Nor is the fear that Islamic schools could, in certain circumstances, contribute to ghettoization completely fanciful. My argument is that this is only one possible outcome and, here, as elsewhere, we cannot abstain from action because of the risk that the results of that action will not be those we wish. There is also the opposite and, I believe, more persuasive view that this is a profoundly sensible way of furthering the goal of an open and genuinely pluralistic society, in which the aspirations of faith communities are publicly recognized as being able to contribute positively towards the greater social good. This view is, of course, premised on the acceptance of the present *status quo* as being the historical starting-point. Naturally, the model of church–state relations applied in this situation cannot be transferred into other situations, and reflects a uniquely British way of resolving a problem that others address in different terms, because they start from a different base, with different assumptions. The principle of pluralism applies not only within but also between nations and, I am suggesting, is as conducive to the openness and well-being of society as the principle that freedom and secularization constitute, in every case, a common cause. The history of the twentieth century should, at the very least, have demonstrated that this latter principle is highly questionable – yet it continues to retain an extraordinary, unwarranted and largely unexamined prestige.

We may seem to have digressed from the question as to the place of thinking about God in church and academy, but the points we have been considering can readily be applied to that question. For our discussion suggests that, on the basis of what has been said about the end of theology, it would be premature (and inconsistent with the tone of my general reflections on the varieties of church/state relations) to demand the unqualified exclusion of faith commitments from the task of helping to shape the discourse on religion and on God as the ultimate object of religion that is conducted in higher teaching and research. And after all, it might be said, religion is not the only case in which the academy admits non-academic practices into its own life. Fields as diverse as medicine and fine art provide examples of two-track approaches to the interweavings of theory and practice, in which the role of the practitioners is acknowledged as having a legitimate place within the overall configuration of academic life. No less than society itself, the academy is a complex institutional space that draws strength from this very complexity. To apply the guillotine in such a way as to reduce its life to the functioning of a merely theoretical institution, 'academic' in the narrow sense, would be to diminish not only its vital plurality but also its freedom.

Again, I do not wish to be read as saying more than I am saying, and these remarks cannot be taken as an automatic endorsement of each and every current way of arranging these things. Where we are now is where we have evolved to, and this evolution is both historical and local. There is not only room for legitimate variations between nations, there is also considerable scope for variations between individual universities, according to their own specific history and circumstances. But, no less importantly, we should be all the more alert to the possibility that particular solutions to local problems become separated from their original context and can live on to obstruct and thwart the solution of contemporary problems. Neither antiquity nor curiosity can of themselves justify the perpetuation of institutional arrangements that no longer serve the needs of teaching, learning or research, even if they do so in the name of religion.

However, the acceptance of the view that faith communities can justify their presence in the larger life of the academy does not of itself justify the perpetuation of the right of confessional theology to exist as an academic subject. Is it not rather the case that, if theology is obliged to meet the same criteria of evidence and argument as all other disciplines, it in effect becomes religious studies, a humanistic science? As such it cannot claim any privileged knowledge as to the Being of beings that would be denied to any other comparable science, since its specific resources (scripture and tradition) are not binding upon other disciplines, and in going beyond these it has no methodology at its disposal that it does not share with others. If it identifies itself in confessional terms, it limits itself by definition to the beliefs and values of the community it serves. It can say that *this* is what the community should believe, and *these* are the consequences that flow from the belief for those committed to it, etc., but it cannot, within the limits of academic discourse, say that these beliefs require assent from those in other faith communities or in other fields or that the uncommitted are bound by the same imperatives of action. Lutheran theology can explain why Lutherans regard the Catholic view of the relationship between faith and works as flawed: it cannot require non-Lutherans to accept their way of setting the argument up. Still less can such a theology insist upon the literary critic or nuclear physicist accepting its defining questions as in any way determinative for their own research. Such an insistence could not be experienced as anything other than heteronomy in our contemporary situation. Committed theology can generate fruitful and provocative interpretations of texts and events: it cannot answer for its own status within the wider economy of higher education.

Let me expand these comments by revisiting the crude distinction I drew at the start of this chapter between theology in the church and theology in the academy. There, it will be recalled, I drew attention to how a church-based theology might find expression in talking about 'how to pray', whilst an academic theologian might be more interested in asking about the concept of prayer. We can, of course, explain this difference in terms of the difference between 'practice' and 'theory', and say that whereas theology in the church is driven by the urgency of practice, theology in the academy takes the more leisurely route of theory. There is some force in this – but, at the same time, it obscures what both types of theology have in common.

We may begin by observing that instructing the faithful in 'how to pray' is not simply an unreflective, spontaneous expression of a 'practical' commitment to Christian living. Such instruction is never (one hopes) going to be given without some prior reflection as to the nature of prayer, the kind of contexts in which it is appropriate to pray, and the various forms and ways of praying available to believers. 'Practice' is never mere 'action', but the putting into practice of a kind of understanding that embraces both self and world. That is precisely why it is appropriate to speak of 'theology' even at what might be regarded as quite low levels of intellectual culture in the life of the church. Even though it is often said that Christianity is caught not taught, it is never caught in the way we catch a disease, i.e., without our consideration or approval. The power of example is perhaps the most powerful instrument of Christian persuasion, but the example does not exert its power in a magical way: the example must be understandable as well as affecting, and when the human propensity for imitative behaviour is indulged without reflection we are underway to the loss of self that is characteristic of the mob and that, as René Girard has so eloquently shown, can so rapidly lead to the wildest excesses of collective irrationalism. The language of even the simplest, most unlettered believer is always going to involve some element of reflection, judgment and interpretation and is, thus far, 'theological'. Nonetheless, what is said about prayer in the church context is going to be said differently from what is said in the academic context.

But this difference is not merely one of complexity or abstraction, and church theology is, in its own terms, frequently no less complex or abstract than what is said by the neutral 'science' of religious studies.

Nonetheless there is a difference. But in what does it consist? Perhaps we can put it like this: theology as practised in the church has the character of rhetoric, understood precisely in Aristotle's sense as the art of persuasion, an art that has an intrinsic relation to ethical and political practice. Theology in the church concerns what needs to be said in order to persuade those to whom it is addressed to adopt the Christian faith and to incorporate into their lives the modes of action (including, of course, such 'action' as prayer) that belong to it. To speak of it in this way is not to deny that there are important differentiations within theology, differentiations that mark out the professor of systematic theology from the homespun revivalist. The differences, however, fall within a common field whose boundaries are determined by the exigencies of persuasion. As an 'art', the practice of rhetoric is not immediately dependent on higher-order knowledge, any more than a great painter or actor need have a developed critical or historical knowledge of their respective arts. Nonetheless, an art is, as such, never purely naive, and the concept of art goes some way towards meeting the force of my comments about the necessarily reflective nature of even the simplest faith. Art always embodies a certain understanding of the world; it is always the articulation of an interpretation, even though the practitioner of an art may give relatively little time to higher-order theoretical reflections on its method or meaning. Church theology develops such reflection, and in doing so accepts that its scope is prescribed in advance by the requirements of the practical art of Christian persuasion, the cause of persuading the world of its faith.

But if theology is in this way defined in a fundamental way by the need of faith-communities to develop a self-interpretation appropriate to the demands of confession and discipleship, how can it answer for the truth of the message outside the orbit of those communities? Is theology, as some have said, purely inter-textual? If so, then it might be able to justify the content of faith in the sense of showing that believers are not incoherent or inconsistent or without reason in holding their faith to be true, and it might well be able to generate more generous, more inclusive presentations of the faith that is believed – but it cannot show that this faith has any validity for those outside the fold. If theology wishes to assert itself as a body of truth-claims that require and deserve the attention of non-theologians and non-believers, then it can only do so along the way of dialogue. The truth of religion cannot be decided without engaging in the always piecemeal and necessarily open-ended enquiry as to what religion means in relation to natural, social, political or historical science, or to literature, fine art or philosophy. In the nature of the case, however, such dialogue cannot be the exclusive province of theology in the traditional sense, and this means that theology must surrender the claim to be judge in its own cause. Church theology cannot itself define in advance what questions are or are not admissible in the pursuit of a truthful thinking about God. There are no unearned credits. Moreover, because the dialogical process is one that is in principle never-ending, theology must also learn to live with the uncertainty of a situation in which the jury is for ever 'out' and final judgment is for ever suspended. Paradoxically, however, it is precisely when theology is willing to do this that it makes good its claim to be a part of the academy, since such mutual interrogation is integral to the freedom of enquiry that is of the very essence of academic life. The demand to expel confessional theology from the academy and confine it to the restricted domain of the church will rise and fall in intensity precisely in line with theology's refusal or acceptance of such dialogue.

Indeed, the situation of theology in this respect is not dissimilar to that of some other disciplines or sub-disciplines. Take Marxism and deconstruction, as two very different (though not unrelated) examples. In the one case we have a whole world-view and body of practices, in the other a critical procedure. Each has had a massive impact on work in the humanities and social sciences, and each has provoked considerable resistance and, often, downright hostility. In the face of the criticism levelled against them by colleagues, Marxists and deconstructionists face a simple choice. Either they refuse dialogue, retreating into an enclave of like-minded believers, with the result that they produce works that are ever more esoteric, ever more incredible and ever more marginalized – or they allow themselves to be challenged, responding creatively to criticism and facilitating an exchange in which the price of acceptance into the mainstream of public discourse is the willingness to revise their own positions. It is only when the necessity of dialogue is embraced that such movements in ideas have been able to contribute positively to the development of human self-understanding – and it is no different for theology. Purists may shout 'Sell-out!', but, as in politics, purists tend to define themselves out of existence.

But who is to see to it that this dialogue takes place? Who is to act as referee? Who is to be judge? Are we invoking some meta-discipline that, lacking a field of its own, is nonetheless competent to prescribe and to regulate the boundaries of others?

This would seem implausible, since, as has been said, the kind of dialogue that is being looked for must take place simultaneously along a multiplicity of fronts: it will be a dialogue with science *and* with literature, with sociology *and* with epistemology. In each case the specifics of the local situation will determine the shape, method and outcome of the dialogical process, and will also be affected by the other disputes and dialogues being conducted by the other discipline concerned: theology's dialogue with literature, for example, cannot be sealed off from concurrent debates between literature and social theory or literature and philosophy. It is therefore obvious that the terrain of contemporary academic life is going to be too varied, and its political map too Byzantine, for any master-discipline to impose any universal solutions.

Today, not even philosophy is in a position to arrogate to itself the role of universal science, the science of sciences, since the kind of overview that would be necessary to bring the whole field of scientific endeavour into the frame of a single point of view is as much beyond the grasp of philosophical method as it is beyond that of theology. Philosophy has no more right than theology to police the multitude of inter-disciplinary boundaries that divide the landscape of the contemporary academy, nor has it the authority to be a court of appeal with regard to any boundary disputes. But if it cannot impose binding arbitration, it can nonetheless assist those who meet at the boundaries between disciplines to understand the meaning of the other. If it is not understood in terms of a homogeneous, unified discipline, but as a self-transforming body of case-law and of accumulated experience in dealing with inter-disciplinary debates, then philosophy may be able to provide something of what is needed. In this sense we may say that it provides a kind of translation service to the academy. But this is too weak, since philosophy not only offers assistance, it also challenges and requires each discipline to be alert to the outstanding obligation of mutual intelligibility that is a necessary condition of communal living within a pluralistic, multi-disciplined university. Not just a translation service but a kind of Amnesty International or Charter 88 of the world of ideas, philosophy has the potential to serve as the conscience of the contemporary academy. In this sense, it will be in and as the philosophy of religion that the claims of religion to offer a more than provincial meaning and truth are best articulated, tried and tested and the question of God takes shape as a question that is important and meaningful in our time and place.

If the philosophy of religion can in this way draw theology into the kind of dialogue it needs to be involved in if it is to survive, it must itself cede control of the dialogical process beyond a certain point. Its task is to facilitate, not to command. The philosophy of religion must always dissolve into the concrete dialogical task of relating the claims and symbols of specific faith-communities to one or other specific discourse. It will, therefore, inevitably overflow the constraints of philosophy of religion as a single, unified academic subject: not so much a discipline – a body of knowledge and methods – but a kind of intellectual readiness, on perpetual stand-by for the moment when local boundaries become suddenly and unexpectedly significant and controversial, and disputes flare up with the unpredictability of regional wars. But it should be added that as soon as the debates that develop at these flash-points move beyond mere polemics, they are themselves underway to becoming 'philosophical' in a broad sense. They do not need to wait upon the arrival of philosophers of religion to certify that their discussions are genuinely dialogical. The name 'philosophy' of itself carries no more intrinsic authority than does 'theology'.

Theology, if it is to continue as a part of the academy (and nothing I have said should be interpreted as implying that it will not so continue), must, then, submit to the discipline of dialogue. But what of theology in the church? Do seminaries and synods have any obligations apart from those they have to their own members? Cannot revelationism or narrative theologies be left in peace, as long as they confine themselves to the internal life of the church, debating amongst themselves what needs to be said for the furtherance and maintenance of the church's cause?

Perhaps, if they wished to do so, then they should indeed be allowed to depart in peace – but they would have to be warned that they were indeed 'departing' from the common life of academy and society. In fact, for the most part, they show little inclination to go. Indeed, as already suggested, there is an internally-generated drive within faith communities towards involvement with the wider society, a drive that brings with it the need to make their vision of the world intelligible to their neighbours. Any social involvement is going to bring with it the obligation of dialogue, however minimal, and dialogue brings with it the obligation to listen as well as to speak. It will not often look like what is currently practised under the heading 'philosophy of religion', but whenever such dialogue occurs there is a kind of philosophizing about religion going on, and a more or less articulated reflection on the question as to what it is that makes the aims and claims of the faith community intelligible to its social or intellectual neighbours. Only a community that could effect a total withdrawal from the world would be able to dispense with such dialogue, and although such ambitions are embraced by some religious groups and individuals, their manner of refusing dialogue of itself inures them to the consequences of such renunciation. It can, however, safely be said that any theologian, no matter how 'revelationist' in principle, who publishes through a mainstream publishing house and holds a university office thereby reveals a desire to be 'in', even when 'not of', the world. The condition of being 'in', however, is to expose the 'vertical' world of faith to the 'horizontal' world of dialogue, and to expose doctrine to the test of philosophy.

If the principle of dialogue functions in the academy as a means of securing the integration of theology into the discursive process of academic life, it correspondingly serves the church by preventing doctrine from imploding. Unless the church is willing and able to subject its own theoretical and practical life to the rigour of disciplined self-reflection, (i.e., by 'philosophizing' upon its own truth claims and practices), it will suffer a kind of organismic entropy, its vibrant, dynamic complexity being reduced to a mono-culture of ever-increasing inertia. To achieve the self-reflection needed to do this, believers will have to acquire the ability to establish an imaginative distance from their own beliefs and to look upon themselves as if with the eyes of others. And if this sounds like wilful make-believe, the illusion is only apparent. For modern believers are, inevitably, participants in worlds and forms of life that are larger far than the worlds of church and theology. We don't have to pretend to be 'outsiders', since every one of us is, simultaneously, an 'outsider/insider'. Even those who most insist on their orthodoxy have usually lived or continue to live in some parts of their lives outside the reservations of church and theology. Their very orthodoxy may well bear the mark of a disappointed engagement with 'the world'. The will to become orthodox can even be said to be one very 'modernist' way of existentially interpreting the condition of modernity.

Theology and thinking about God: society and the individual

Much has already been said by way of implication about the individual as one of the significant sites of contemporary thinking about God, but before turning to examine this in more detail, I shall, briefly and inadequately, consider the role played by the life of society in determining the form that thinking about God will take for our time.

In the middle of the twentieth century, Paul Tillich proposed that theology should commit itself to what he called a method of correlation, arguing that it was the theologian's task to formulate the 'question' posed by the world in such a way as to allow the theological 'answer' to be heard. Although Tillich was also concerned with the kind of dialogue between academic disciplines I have been discussing, he was no less concerned with a range of issues, being, at different times, particularly engaged in exploring the correlations between Christianity and Marxism, psycho-analysis, modern art and existentialism. Times change, of course, and the contemporary social situation offers a different (though not absolutely different) range of situations and movements that call for dialogue.

I am, for example, writing this on the eve of the annual Oscar ceremony. This event now attracts a level of interest and publicity (including live coverage on British television) far beyond what it had a generation ago, when many pundits were confidently predicting the early demise of the cinema and its supersession by video. It is surely no coincidence that film is simultaneously becoming a focus of reflection in academic theology, where what was once a mere trickle of articles is turning into a continuous stream of articles, books, dissertations and conferences.

At another level, the real and extreme urgency of the environmental crisis confronting all human communities has made 'green' issues an important focus of theological reflection for a number of years. As in other areas of Christian ethics, this reflection has not merely been about the deduction of imperatives for Christian action from the indicatives of Christian doctrine. It has also fed back into a re-examination of the tradition itself, a re-examination that has, on the one hand, subjected aspects of the tradition to repentant self-criticism and, on the other, retrieved a range of neglected or forgotten resources well-suited to the devotional, practical and doctrinal needs of the present.

Something similar could also be said about the impact of feminism. Despite the sadly undeniable history of the church's connivance in millennia of injustice towards women, Christianity might more plausibly claim to have generated proto-feminist movements than to have been a proto-green pressure group (especially if we take heterodox or marginal Christian movements into account). Here too there has been both self-criticism, often deservedly harsh, and the recovery of lost or suppressed voices, with important and substantial revisions of Christian history and self-understanding. Nonetheless, even though this task is something to which theology *could* have been led by considering its own internal agenda, it is in fact extremely implausible to claim that the flood-gates would have been opened without the pressure of feminism in the wider society in which theology and the church live and operate.

I have picked out three areas where contemporary society is powerfully impacting on theology, and the list could be continued almost indefinitely, adding science, politics, economics and many other complexes of issues that have become a part of the landscape of modern religious thought.

It might well be starting to sound as if I regard the agenda of theology as completely dependent on the outside world. Those who embraced Tillich's method of correlation were easily accused of surrendering all theological integrity, and encouraging a situation in which theology simply trailed along behind whatever trends were perceived to engage the ephemeral attention of the chattering classes. However, it should be clear that dialogue is not the same as reductionism. If theology does not possess an 'answer' that exists for itself and by itself in some abstract non-dialogical space, it should never allow itself to be the mere reflection of its environment. Dialogue is only ever dialogue if it is between partners who are genuinely different and irreducible.

Of course there is a way of dealing theologically with film, feminism and green issues that seems to be no more than Sunday supplement journalism dressed up in the language of scripture and tradition. But if we reduce the issues themselves to their representation in the mass media, then we are trivializing things that, in very different ways, reveal important aspects of human being today. They do not grip our attention merely because they are trendy, but because we recognize them as moulding the very form of the life we now live. Nor should we think of the world setting the agenda in the manner of a smart company chairman who knows how to use the agenda to determine the outcome of the meeting. The issues do not demand our attention and require interpretation because they come with ready-made answers or constrain our life-possibilities. It is rather that they become issues for us precisely because they either resist or cannot be exhausted by our efforts to understand them. It is their enigmatic and inexhaustible character that makes them the fitting focus for thinking about God, for they point towards the questionability of our prevailing self-images, and preserve the possibility of a transcendence we have not yet mastered or absorbed.

These comments provide another angle on my preference for the expression 'thinking about God' as against 'theology'. For 'theology' summons up the idea of a determinate body of doctrine, within which we are to find the 'answer' to the world's 'question'. But the agenda of theology can no more determine the outcome of dialogue than that of the world. Indeed, the dialogical approach does not presuppose that the 'answer' in any way pre-exists the 'question'. It is rather as if the religious tradition, on the one hand, and the world, on the other, were the flintstones that, when struck, generate a spark of understanding, a glimmer of meaning, that is quite different in kind and character than either. To speak of this understanding and this meaning as the 'answer' is to speak in a rough and ready way. Perhaps it would be better to speak of it as a new 'question' – not so as to lure us down the path of agonizing existential navel-gazing, but as a question that blazes a trail from present to future, suffusing the enigma of our present darkness with the glow of hope: hope that wisdom is, if not attained, still worth pursuing. In this light, even the expression 'thinking *about* God' seems too limiting, and should, perhaps, be reformulated as 'thinking *towards* God'.[3]

It is also misleading to suggest that religion only ever arrives on the scene after the world has formulated its questions and set its agenda. It is often like this, sometimes embarrassingly so – as when the church signals its incomprehension of the world precisely by the inappropriateness of its attempt to address the world in its own terms and be relevant (like the 'swinging vicars' of the 1960s who seemed to believe that the use of expressions like 'Jesus is cool' or 'God is groovy' would ingratiate them with counter-cultural youth). But it doesn't have to be like that, and there have, even within the modern period, been religious thinkers who have not waited upon the world to draw up its questions but have shown that they themselves have been tested in the crucible in which the questions are formed. Such thinkers (in my judgment) would include Schleiermacher, Kierkegaard, Dostoevsky, Unamuno, Buber, Marcel, Eliot and Auden (and perhaps also Tillich, Teilhard de Chardin and the early Barth, but with important

---

[3] See the comments about the distinction between my dialogism and that of Buber in Chapter 2 above, also about the role of the future in thinking about God in Chapter 3 above.

qualifications). In each case these are individuals who have stood at the epicentre of the shattering earthquakes that have marked the course of modernity, and thought about God out of the turmoil of that situation. In each case, also, they have not merely contributed to 'theology' in the narrow sense, but have helped to transform the agenda and questions of the world and of 'secular' thinking. They well illustrate the truth that genuine thinking about God does not belong in the realm of secondariness, but is itself thinking that addresses the heart of the matter. Only a few will ever achieve the stature of the thinkers I have listed, but my point is not about 'greatness'. There have been many theologians in the modern era no less intellectually gifted and no less productive than these, whose work has, nonetheless, had the stamp of secondariness. Equally, there are many of average and even poor ability who have, in a qualitative sense, been 'original', whose thinking about God has been formed in the light of their own experiences and their own judgments and who have courageously assumed responsibility for the positions at which they have arrived, even if doctrinally and ethically they remained within existing paradigms of thought and action.

However, we should not assume that the question of theology's relation to the wider society in which it is set is exhausted by addressing the issues that are of concern to that society. There is also another way of looking at this relationship that focusses not so much on issues as on identifying the kind of social space in which theology operates.

Indeed, it has to be acknowledged that prioritizing the question of theology in the life of the academy already provides a seductive but questionable 'placing' of religion in society. Although it comes seemingly naturally to see educational institutions as a primary site for thinking about God, such a perception presupposes a number of assumptions about the nature of those institutions and, indeed, the nature of thinking about God. It already suggests a bias towards the view that religion somehow belongs to the 'theoretical' pole of life together with the belief that the university has some kind of monopoly on thinking. Both these assumptions, however, are themselves the fruits of a culture shaped by metaphysical assumptions. There are in fact many other social sites in which God gets thought about, although often in ways scarcely recognizable to those schooled in mainstream theology and philosophy. The cultures of politics, business and the arts are, amongst others, richly seamed with explorations and interpretations of existence that are often implicitly and sometimes explicitly religious, nor are these without the ability to be self-critical with regard to their religious element. It is just that, for the most part, they speak a strange language that those who think about God in the context of the academy have not yet learned to read, except in a fumbling and stuttering way. The hard truth that those in the academy are going to have to learn (and are, perhaps, beginning so to do) is that the instruments with which they seek to map the cognitive topography of today's complex social space are still in a very early stage of development. Heidegger notoriously praised the clear vision of the Black Forest farmer as revelatory of a kind of thinking that those caught up in the chatter of academic philosophy have not yet attained. The example is, perhaps, sentimental and, unfortunately, politically sensitive, but it does indicate an awareness that thinking can never be the monopoly of any self-defining cadre.[4] The same point could, after all, be made in virtually opposite terms if, following Harvey Cox's celebration of 'the secular city', we were to recognize 'the city' as constituting a distinctive social site that generates its own distinctive family of styles of thinking. The country and the city thus provide a preliminary hint as to how the consideration of social space might expand our awareness of what conditions and constrains yet also fructifies thinking. The use of

---

[4] The same point might be made, perhaps less controversially, by considering the way in which contemporary thought encounters the thinking of pre-modern peoples, or deals with the various species of what might be called 'unofficial knowledge' that linger in the neglected back streets of modern culture.

such spatial categories in interpreting the subject matter of humanistic science is, however, very much in its infancy, with Walter Benjamin's work on Baudelaire's Paris providing the best-known example, albeit one that is more suggestive than conclusive. Unfortunately little or no theology has yet ventured into this domain.[5]

It has already been remarked that the contextualization of theology is not exhausted by the question of its social contexts, but also embraces the category of the individual. Many will find this a natural progression, but for others it is likely to seem immensely controversial. Just as the identification of intellectual freedom with progressive secularization is presupposed in many parts of the academy, so too is the assumption that, for the purposes of adequate theorization, 'the individual' is a bankrupt category.

This assumption is fed, in theology as elsewhere, by diverse but convergent streams. On the one hand there is a philosophical line that derives from a Wittgensteinian view of language, where it is axiomatic that there is no such thing as a private language and that theological statements do not express the feelings or commitments of individuals any more than they refer to objective entities in the world: they are what they are only in and through their contextualization in the larger language game and form of life of which they are a part. A quite different source is provided by Marxian and other social and political approaches (including some forms of feminism), for which the emphasis on the individual or the personal involves a mystification of the real structures of meaning and value in society. The existentialist viewpoint that locates the origin of meaning and value in the individual, justifying itself by anecdotal appeals to introspection, simply absolutizes a perspectival illusion

---

[5] This is undoubtedly because much twentieth-century theology has been preoccupied with questions of history and has, in theologians as diverse as Tillich and Cullmann, consistently privileged the categories of temporality over those of space. 'Spatiality' continues to be the target of some contemporary theological polemics.

that inheres in the individual standpoint, just as human beings seem to see the sun cross the sky from east to west. Reality is a social construct, not a private passion. This critique of the individual, and the accompanying emphasis upon the structural dimensions of sin, alienation and injustice, has penetrated many areas of theological reflection, including pastoral care and liturgics, where what are regarded as the defunct individualistic models are seen as having contributed to the prevalence of the ills they sought to make good. The pastor whose hospital visit brings consolation to the patient is actually working against the good if he ignores the structural evil of the unequal availability of health care and the business and political pressures that determine which treatments are available for which illnesses and for which patients. To the Wittgensteinian, Marxian and sociological ways of demoting the individual, we must also add the diffusion of the view, often ascribed to Derrida (and, more broadly, to 'postmodernism'), that there is no reality, only representation: there is nothing but language, and language, because its true character is better reflected in writing than in living speech, is not a personal or subjective means of self-expression but a self-propagating system – language has killed the author. Finally, we may add that, in the manner of some *éminence grise*, theology still has authoritarian voices whispering against the expression of individual dissent, since it is in the institution alone, the Church with a very big capital 'C', that truth resides and it is only by conforming ourselves to the truth of the Church that we can know of any truth at all.

These various ways of critiquing an earlier generation's emphasis on the individual do, of course, differ amongst themselves. Some Marxists and some postmodernists are as bitter foes as you could look to find. On the other hand, the extraordinary complexity of contemporary culture means that we sometimes find several of these strands (perhaps, on occasion, all of them) woven into a single theological line.

Now I do not wish to deny that (with the exception of my imaginary *éminence grise*) each of these ways of critique have something of value to offer. What I contest is whether, singly or collectively, they establish an adequate or complete picture of the human condition and, specifically, of the human religious condition. Clearly, as a corrective to some versions of extreme individualism (as reflected in Mrs Thatcher's famous remark that there is no such thing as society) they are important. But they too can be charged with mystifying crucial aspects of our being human.

I accept that, as a language-user, I am born into certain cultural traditions and occupy a social space defined by the circumstances of my birth, gender, race, class and profession, and that all my thoughts, words and deeds are permeated by their social mediations. Consequently, I cannot aspire to any kind of objective self-knowledge that by-passes the whole complex of such mediations. This does not, however, mean that I have to accept the reductionist hypothesis that gets smuggled in under the protection of this situation. Even if I accept that my very body is, to an extent much greater than I customarily imagine, a social construct, I have also to accept that it is the product of physical, chemical and biological processes. Acceptance of the social construction of the body, however, does not require me to abandon the claim that the human subject is to be treated with the dignity and respect implied by the term 'personality' any more than does acceptance of its physical determination. If an objective understanding of human being must take all these factors into account, such an understanding (that is, in any case, far from complete) cannot absolve me from pursuing the kind of self-knowledge and undertaking the kind of moral and social actions that are only possible on the basis of my individuality and subjectivity. Because I cannot do everything, it does not follow that I cannot do something, and because the something I can do will only mitigate the ill-effects of the system, not overthrow it, does not mean that it is not worth doing. Because health-care as we know it is systematically unequal does not mean that those in its care (many of whom might be dead in a few days) should be refused the consolation of someone who will listen to them, counsel them or just be with them as individuals, one-to-one. Because I live in

Germany in 1944 and have no opportunity, as an individual, to influence the murderous policy of the regime, it does not follow that I should not risk my life to shelter my Jewish neighbour. Even when we know that we are but crying in the wilderness and our voices are fated to be lost on the wind, there are situations in which we must speak and act and suffer – even if, from the standpoint of prudence and social theory, it is 'for nothing'. Sometimes, indeed, our subjectivity may not even find the means or the occasion of crying out. Sometimes all that I have is silence and suffering, and then, even if I know that there have been too many victims who have kept silent and suffered when they should have risen up in revolt, keeping silent and suffering becomes my way, my unique, life-engaging, life-demanding way of posing the question of God.[6] We might think of Simone Weil – '*toujours Antigone*' – and if this example might seem to corroborate the suspicion that excessive individualism is pathological, Weil remains the creator of some of the most original, most penetrating and most delicate of modern writings on the spiritual life.

We are talking extreme cases, and certainly do not need to go that far to establish the claim of the individual to be one of the constitutive sites of thinking about God. That moral anguish and moral action cannot ever but be the anguish and the action of individuals is of itself an important argument. Whether to consent to my partner's wish for euthanasia, whether to resign my post on a matter of principle, whether to fight for my country, whether to get married . . . all such issues, whilst deeply interwoven with structures of society that far transcend my private situation, are issues that present me with questions that only I can resolve. The same

---

[6] These comments also point back to the discussion in Chapter 1 of the fact that dialogue, as that is conceived here, is not confined to an elite of ideal-speech practitioners. Dialogue is actual whenever it is made actual in the lives of individuals, including marginal individuals and groups who are excluded from the dominant discourses of their society and whose voices are not heard, except by themselves. Here too we should recall the eschatological horizon briefly sketched at the end of Chapter 3.

can be said, with perhaps greater emphasis, with regard to my moral failings and my mortality. Here too I am involved in situations and questions that individualize me absolutely – not in the sense that they take me out of the world I share with others or allow me to slip the chain of dialogue, but in the sense that, in the moment when these situations and these questions claim my attention, I become the place, the site, at which the dialogue becomes actual. In so far as the way of dialogue is devoted to revealing the presence of the personal at the heart of life, things cannot be otherwise. Although the personal is not and cannot be reduced to the individual, it is unthinkable without the individual. If the individual voice is absorbed without remainder into the discourse of academy, church and society, the word of dialogue can never be spoken, and the possibility of affirming the value, dignity and, even, sanctity of the person will be pre-emptively denied. If such a denial is characteristic of powerful currents in our technological society, it must be opposed. For although the methods and rhetoric of contemporary domination and control are benign in comparison with those of the era of totalitarianism, their logic is no less totalitarian and their rhetoric is no less conducive to minimizing the aspirations to personhood that, I am convinced, only the language and symbols of religion can fitfully, enigmatically and remotely express.

We have, then, explored the time and the space of thinking about God, but we are not finished. It would be easy to assume from everything said so far that thinking about God is coterminous with the thinking about God that occurs in and by means of language. That, however, is not the case. Although this remains one of the prejudices of thinking that is hardest to dispel, we must nonetheless seek to address it. Because I am neither an artist nor a musician, nor yet a mystic, my attempt to identify, challenge and unsettle this prejudice will, paradoxically, be made in language, and (what's more) the prose of one who writes in the academic style. It is a paradox, and it is unsatisfactory. Just how paradoxical and how unsatisfactory is up to the reader to judge.

5

Beyond Words

Language and its limits

For much of this book, I may appear to have assumed that thinking about God is exclusively a matter of words. The very etymology of 'theology' suggests that, whatever may go on elsewhere in the domain of religion, what we are concerned with here is the 'logos', the 'word' or discourse about God conducted in words and aimed at speaking rightly about God. Nor is this just a point of etymology. The whole history of theology corroborates this way of conceiving of the subject. The great crises of theology – the debates that culminated in the Creed of Nicaea, the Protestant Reformation and its return to the biblical Word as the sole source of right doctrine, the arguments about papal authority and liturgical reform – have turned on verbal forms and usages, on what can rightly be said about the matter in hand. Right belief has, almost invariably, been understood in terms of assenting to a specific, verbally articulated proposition or set of propositions. What the faith 'is' and what we can say that the faith 'is' have been treated as virtually indistinguishable. Not that any of the major figures of the tradition would want to say that it's all just a matter of words. On the contrary, the assumption has been that getting the words right is important precisely because language has to do with reality and that the propositions to which our sentences give shape define a line of vision that must be as precise as possible if we are to see that specific aspect of reality at which the proposition aims. Some modern theologies would go further and say that reality itself is word-shaped, because 'Word' is the fundamental category in and through which God Himself 'deals with' His world. The primary 'object' of theology is not 'God' as some kind of metaphysical object, but God revealed in and through His Word. Theology, then, becomes the business of fitting our fumbling human words to the truth of the divine Word that is the sole source and criterion of all reality as well as of all right speaking.

The assumption that the words of theologians mean what they mean because of their relation to a putative 'reality' reflected in or denoted by them is, however, a further exemplification of the metaphysical prejudices of ontology. Unfortunately (unfortunately, that is, for those who hold to this prejudice) not even our most careful verbal formulations can constrain the way things really are. Every formulation, every practice or body of practices is, on the principle of dialogism expounded in this book, open to revision and, if necessary, wholesale replacement. Because dialogue is in perpetual motion, there is no right way of talking, no sempiternal language of revelation that is not subject to the transformative process of dialogue. It follows that even those credal formulations that supposedly define the faith of the church cannot be preserved for ever from the dynamics of history. It is in this respect striking how, in the last couple of generations, the so-called Athanasian Creed has virtually fallen out of use in the Church of England, whilst revisions of both the Nicene and Apostles' Creeds for liturgical use have involved some alteration to the meaning of what is confessed. Even a minimalist formula such as 'Jesus is Lord' cannot be regarded as having some trans-historical sense, unless it is supplemented by a body of interpretation that sets forth how the first-century connotations of Lordship can meaningfully be re-appropriated in contemporary terms (and what those contemporary terms would be).

But dialogue is, of course, also a 'logos'-word. Indeed, it could be objected that 'dialogue' involves a far more thorough-going identification of thinking about God with thinking about God in language than traditional theology ever did. I have already acknowledged the likelihood that some will see in the version of dialogism presented here just a recipe for talk, talk and more talk. At least theologians of the old school believed that their words related in some way or other to a more-than-linguistic reality, and that they had a responsibility towards truths that were independent of their own attempts to express them. Language was privileged over all other media of communication and symbolism, but only on the condition that it was in the service of reality.

My position, by way of contrast, might seem to veer towards that of those (neo-conservative) theologians who argue that theology is simply a matter of textuality, a self-contained language-game whose rules are defined by the players themselves and that has no need to engage with the 'extra-textual' discoveries about the world being made by historians and scientists. Or perhaps it may be seen as more akin to that (radical) theology in which the world itself has become absorbed into language, and reality itself is nothing but language, the sum of its representations. Either way, thinking about God seems to have been set free from the awkward and arduous business of checking out the words it uses against what is generally taken to be the 'real' world, 'out there' beyond the boundaries of language.

Dialogism does, of course, sound like yet another ideology of language, an academic word-child's excuse for indulging the verbal proficiency that is his *métier*. I have, however, already disowned that view of language that regards meaning and use as constrained by etymology. The primordial aura of words has long since paled in the light of their subsequent history and use, and although it matters that we aim at significant continuity in the way we use words (because if not, we soon become incomprehensible), the vital thing is that we are clear as to how we are, in fact, using them now. Thus, although I have repeatedly spoken of dialogue in such a way as to suggest that this is essentially a verbal interaction, whether it be a conversation or a mutual interrogation, it needs to be said that language is only one level at which dialogue operates. It would obviously be foolish to deny that for us human beings language is enormously important. In and through language we declare our love and faith, bind ourselves in marriage, frame laws, pronounce judgment and seek wisdom. But that is not the same as saying that language is the only factor operative in all these uses. Even if it is only through the speaking or the writing of the word that a state of affairs can be enacted (as in the marriage ceremony or the pronouncement of a judicial sentence), it does not follow that what language 'does' can be isolated from the whole context in which it is used. That it is this man and this woman or this judge who speaks these particular words at this particular time and in this particular place, against the background of the larger history and context in which all of this occurs, is no less important in determining the reality and the meaning of the act accomplished in the words ('I do . . .' or 'I sentence you . . .'). Language itself is the merest tip of the iceberg. If, nonetheless, it is only in language that the situation becomes visible, or acquires social concretion, linguistic meaning still depends on the pre- or extra-linguistic world by which language itself is encompassed and permeated.

But where does this get us? Is it not a truism that 'of that of which we cannot speak, thereof we must keep silent'? What is the point – in a book – of invoking 'the pre- or extra-linguistic' since that, by definition, is precisely what does not and cannot manifest itself in language? Indeed, I have several times drawn attention to the failure of claims concerning non-verbal religious experience to ground anything that could be described as 'knowledge' of God.

Of course there is an obvious sense in which there is no unmediated presence of 'reality' in language. Language, as a system of representation, neither incorporates nor unambiguously points to the world it represents. But this does not mean that language is closed off from the world.

There is a tension here. One side of this is to do with the way in which language transforms the world in such a way that there are no undigested gobbets of 'reality' anywhere within its system of

representation. Even the simplest word of ostensive definition –
'Look there, those things in the field are what I mean by the word
"cow"!' – acts as a kind of alchemical medium in which the object is
no longer embedded in the world out there but re-presented in a
whole new set of contexts and conditions. Baptized by language,
the world changes in such a way that everything remains the same,
yet everything is different. The question is whether this difference
is such as to annihilate all points of contact between the represented
world of language and the 'real' world out there – my view is that it
does not. In saying this, however, it is important not to confuse
different ways of conceptualizing the relationship between language and reality, or to put the wrong kind of emphasis on the
positive aspect of this relationship.

One way of determining the connections between language and
reality is that of science. Observation, experiment, quantification
and technological application enable science to symbolize the
realities with which it is concerned in a remarkably controlled
manner, such that any assertion or counter-assertion as to what is
the case can be put to the test by agreed methods.

Exactly how science achieves this (that is, exactly how mathe-
matical calculation is, for example, able to predict the existence of
black holes) remains a matter of debate amongst scientists and
philosophers of science. However, that is not our concern here. All
that is necessary for now is to note the fact. For I have already
indicated that the way of contemporary thinking about God is not
in the first instance the way of science. The very means by which
science achieves its astonishing successes have to do with its neglect
of the unobjectifiable, unquantifiable dimension of the personal.
Although the principle of dialogue means that we cannot resign
ourselves to a situation of permanent schizophrenia with regard to
the relationship between science and personalist philosophy (or, to
put it more positively, actively requires us to undertake a repeated
engagement with both science and the philosophy of science), a
dialogical approach to God does not orientate itself in the first
instance with regard to the reality disclosed by science.

Does it then follow that dialogism is pure subjectivism, albeit a kind of subjectivism that is not limited by the narrow boundaries of the individual? It is salutary to remember that Marxists used to speak of their social view of humanity as 'objective' (in opposition to the subjective individualism of bourgeois philosophers), but this did not really make it objective in any sense that would be understood by, say, the natural scientist: in this case 'objective' just meant a kind of corporate subjectivity. If we have already decided that any kind of discourse that is not that of science is merely subjective, then we will indeed conclude that dialogism is just subjectivism. Even if the dialogist thus accused protests that what he is about is *inter*-subjective, the truly hard-nosed proponent of objectivity will still regard this as a mere variant of subjectivism, rather than a way of transcending it.

Now certainly, dialogism itself would not want to disclaim the importance of subjectivity, since the dialogist has staked his or her own person on the progress and outcome of the dialogical process. This is not just a debate about matters of fact, but a debate about who I am. This 'who I am', however, is not something over which those participating in dialogue have control in the sense that whatever they may happen to agree to at any particular moment is automatically the case. How the question of personal identity (and the question of God that lies coiled within it) is posed at any particular time by the community of those asking it is indeed how the question is now being posed; I have argued that thereby it becomes that form of the question in relation to which I must seek and, having found, testify to my own personal truth. Nonetheless, what is involved here is more than a matter of consensus. For dialogue is itself coloured, conditioned and constrained by factors that are not reducible to the linguistically articulated views and intentions of the participants. As we have already seen, what I bring to the dialogue in terms of the history in which I participate and the concrete circumstances of the site at which dialogue is being conducted work together to focus the otherwise illimitable range of what could possibly be said. Although, perhaps, anything can be said and agreed in principle, and even the wildest flights of dadaistic rhetoric cannot be excluded from the realm of the possibly sayable, in practice it will almost certainly be the case that only those views get an extensive hearing that reflect a serious engagement with their time and place. But it is not just the contingencies of time and place that command the attention of the dialogist. Thus far, we could still be speaking about a purely verbal process. But there is more.

The words we speak are not just the words we choose, nor are they just the words we inherit, nor are they the result of a simple encounter between the *novum* of our contemporary situation and what we have inherited. What other factors – other than the constraints of empirical science – are there? Perhaps we might begin to answer this by reflecting that if human beings are definable as those animals that have language, then it is important to pay attention to the subject as well as to the qualifying term of this definition. Whatever else we are, we are indeed animals, surviving in the world and making a way for ourselves through it with the normal biological and behavioural resources of other animals. Like all other animals we are the products of vast yet intricate cosmic, global and evolutionary processes lasting over billions of years. Whilst it would probably be somewhat romantic to say that we recapitulate the grand narrative of that prehistory in our own lives, it is almost certainly true that it does inform both our bodily capacities for and our behavioural patterns of understanding and self-expression. In other words, before, behind and beneath the language of speech and writing lies an earlier and, in some respects, larger language of communicative processes and practices, a language that ranges from the information exchange of the gene pool through to the movingly eloquent facial, gestural and vocal self-expression of the higher mammals, terrestrial and aquatic. It has often been said of the history of ideas that if we are far-sighted it is because we stand on giants' shoulders, and the same analogy can be applied here: that if human language is able to saturate the landscape of pre-linguistic perception and action as thoroughly as it does, this is only because of the pressure built up over millennia of pre-linguistic evolution. Although language may very well make possible new realms of human self-development and self-understanding, much of its power has to do with its ability to mobilize the resources of the pre-linguistic world.

The literal and the figural

The channels through which the pre-linguistic is able to inform the linguistic are many and various, but it is possible to indicate the kind of area where exchange between the two levels is at its most intimate by referring to what we call 'body-language'. Now clearly, this is an imprecise expression. Although posture and gesture make possible a wide range of communicative behaviour, they do not communicate in the same way as 'language' in the everyday sense. Indeed, in many respects it is quite misleading to call the phenomenon thus named a kind of language at all. Thus, without pre-empting the outcome of debates as to the extent to which body-language is culturally variable – i.e. whether the gestures and facial expressions by which we communicate love or anger are part of our biological inheritance or products of culture – it mostly *seems* to us as if body-language is less variable than language itself. The knotted brows, bulging eyes and scowling mouths of the demons of Buddhist iconography, like the serene smile of the Buddha himself, 'speak' to us with an immediacy that the texts they illustrate lack. Although I probably can't even read a word of the text, I do have some idea as to what is going on in the picture, precisely because of the way in which the image exploits trans-culturally readable gestures and expressions. Or take a photograph like that of the German commander at Stalingrad surrendering to the Russians; you don't need a caption and you don't need to be able to recognize the details of military insignia to know who is surrendering to whom: posture says it all. Even if body-language, like spoken language, is in fact learned, it is learned at a phase in our development or at a level of pre-reflective imitation that makes it seem as if it just comes naturally.[1]

Body-'language' is like yet unlike language; it is analogous to and not a sub-species of language, and analogy, as philosophers have long realized, involves both similarity and dissimilarity. Body-language is like language in that it is a set of communicative practices which express feelings and intentions and with which I can convey information and elicit a response from others. It is unlike language in many ways. As well as those already mentioned we might also consider the extent to which it relies on the immediate presence of the communicating subject and its resistance to the kind of abstraction, generalization and self-referentiality that is integral to language. I can read Shakespeare's plays or listen to them on the radio, and even though I feel I might be missing something by not seeing a live performance (or by not having seen them as played by Shakespeare's own company), I believe that the written or spoken text does give me what is most important in them. On the other hand, I can have only the vaguest sense for what it might have meant to see Nijinsky dance: unless I was there, unless I saw it and experienced it, it is mere report.

Precisely because we are speaking about analogy here, it would be extremely difficult to draw a hard and fast line, and the example of Shakespeare and Nijinsky, masters of the arts of language and of bodily movement and expression respectively, is challengeable in a number of respects. But a hard and fast line is not what I am seeking, since the point is that language is not a hermetically sealed, self-sufficient world unto itself, but draws on and is informed by a

---

[1] On the other hand, just as it is sometimes the case that I don't know which words to use and I have to cast about in my mind for the right word or the right grammatical framework with which to say what I want to say, so too I sometimes find myself unsure whether to smile, to sit up straight, to kneel or to be still. I do make decisions about my use of body-language in a manner analogous to that in which I make decisions regarding my use of language. However, my point is not that body-language *is* innate, but that it *seems* to us to be so, as the sun seems to come up and go down. Whether that really is the case is another matter.

wealth of pre- and extra-linguistic factors. Body-language belongs to a zone of experience in which there is a kind of blending of the inside and the outside of language. This is very much to the benefit of language itself. When I describe a situation to you, I do not need to spell out the meaning expressed in body-language by those involved in the situation. If I say '. . . and you should have seen her blush!' I do not need to add what the blush means. But it is not just in relation to description that body-language serves verbal communication. Everyday speech is riddled with images and metaphors drawn from the realm of bodily life and applied in ways that no longer startle us, because we take them for granted. Yet what does it mean to say that an argument is 'lame', a moral stance (!) is 'upright', that we 'grasp' a concept or have to 'face up to' the consequences of our position? Perhaps we no longer think the original context of such idioms, but if that is so it is surely because they fit so well that we don't notice any impropriety in availing ourselves of them. The figural indwells the literal, enlivening the conventional logic of language with the energy of embodied life.

But although this is familiar to us in the context of everyday conversation (as well as providing the stuff of poetry and creative writing), it is, of course, a source of unease to philosophers and others, like theologians, who are concerned to make language as clear, as perspicuous and as precise as possible. One of philosophy's earliest aims was to ban the poets from the city, or at least to confine their story-telling within the limits prescribed by reason and logic. Subsequently the same impulse has been directed against all figurative and metaphorical elements that are perceived as sources of ambiguity and opacity in the articulation of clear and distinct truths. When they are not seeking to expunge such elements from the language altogether or attempting to create a new language (such as that of symbolic logic), philosophers characteristically require us to pursue a maximal awareness as to when and how what we say is conditioned by figuration, in order to immunize argument and definition against the worst effects of metaphoric impurity.

However, who is to say that the figurative dimension of language is really hostile to truth and clarity of thought? After all, it is almost undeniably the case that much of the great philosophy and theology of the last two and a half thousand years has gained and kept our collective attention precisely because of the boldness of its imaginative vision, its persuasive metaphors and striking similes. Theologians, who long since realized that we sinful human beings cannot know God as He is in Himself, found it relatively easy to accept that there are figures of speech we cannot get behind in talking about God, except by silence. And if philosophers were reluctant to leave it at that, suspecting that the inexpressible was simply a grand word for the vacuous, they too have availed themselves of the resources of figuration in constructing their systems or marshalling their arguments. Descartes introduced his programme for the reform of philosophy by speaking of the desirability of replacing the maze-like shambles of a medieval town with the geometrical order of modern town-planning. Even a philosopher as notorious for the desiccated rigour of his prose as Kant frequently uses images such as the 'secure path' of science and speaks of the province of the understanding as an island 'surrounded by a wide and stormy ocean' in venturing on to which we may be misled by fogs and other murky phenomena into the illusory realms of metaphysics.

The question, of course, is whether such recourse to figurative language is simply a matter of presentation, of winning a hearing for an otherwise unappealing case, or whether it does serious conceptual work. But does the academic distinction between, say, a philosophical and a literary reading of a Kant or a Descartes really do justice to the nature of their actual texts, if we pigeonhole the literary approach as merely having to do with their formal and stylistic aspects? Now, of course, if philosophers avail themselves of a rhetorical or metaphorical flourish as a substitute for argument, then we have every right to challenge them. But is it not sometimes the case that it is precisely the image that best reveals the reach and direction of their arguments? The imaginative moments of a great philosophical text are not in every case to be dismissed as nothing more than stage-setting nor yet to be belittled as mere philosophical legerdemain. Far from concealing the philosopher's intentions, such moments often provide the clearest expression of where he wants to go and why – a point which the references to Descartes and to Kant perfectly illustrate. Philosophers have feared the image because of its power to seduce, to undercut or to by-pass the public business of reason, and of course it can function in this way. But images are only seductive if and when they conceal their own nature and their role in the development of an argument. However, there is no reason why they should not be regarded as an integral part of the public face of the text, promoting its argument in a fully transparent way and thereby open to critical appraisal. But doesn't 'critical appraisal' mean cracking open the shell of the image to reveal the idea within, and moving beyond the figural to a higher level of discourse?

That is certainly how the work of interpretation has often been understood in the past, but abstraction and analysis are not the only ways of responding to the provocation of the figurative. Perhaps the keenest response to an image I believe to be misleading or distorting is to pose a counter-image, a corrective that matches fire with fire. The realm of the figural is, on this understanding, no less welcoming to the principle of dialogue than that of any 'purer' discourse. Against Descartes' evocation of the disorderly chaos of the medieval town, we might set an antithetical picture of the interest and character of such an architectural assemblage, and to Kant's fear that what lies beyond the firm ground of understanding is a foggy and uncertain ocean with indiscernible horizons we might reply by speaking of the dullness of island life and the challenge (and potential rewards) of venturing out into such dangerous waters. The point is that image and metaphor do not only deserve to be given greater attention as *objects* of philosophical scrutiny but also, and more importantly, to be accepted as part of the methodological armoury of critical thinking.

Perhaps the point I am making will become clearer if we consider poetry, since although it is true that philosophers, no less than poets, exploit figuration, this is generally assumed to be the very domain in which the poets are most at home. Now, one way of responding to a poetic work is that of the critical exegete who, quite properly, undertakes to decode the meaning that the poet has delivered to us in the casing of metaphor. As the deed of the hero waits upon the poet, so the word of the poet waits upon the critic. But explanation of this kind is not the only way of responding to poetry.[2] Poets also respond to poets, interpreting their predecessors by allusion, quotation, transformation, parody and innumerable other technical means. Such interpretation is certainly no less intelligent and is very often no less critical or reflective than that of the prose critic (as is exemplified in the fact that the crisis of poetry and the problematization of the poetic imagination has been one of the recurrent leitmotifs of twentieth-century poetry itself). Indeed, it may very well be in the nature of the case that we need a more careful eye, a more patient way of reading, a larger imagination and a greater willingness to suspend judgment in order to follow the inner self-critical dialogue of the poets than is required to learn the prevailing critical or philosophical view concerning the nature and function of literature. However, the fact that a particular manner of thinking is more demanding than what we are used to is no argument against it. It is in this spirit, then, that we plead for philosophy (and, in particular, the philosophy of religion) not to exclude the creative use of figurative language from its methodological resources.

So far we have been considering a kind of interaction between the literal and the figural that stands in the service of language, arguing that the figural is not an element to be banished or expunged but rather a powerful and irreplaceable dimension of linguistic communication that can serve to expand our sense of what is involved in a dialogical approach to thinking about God. Such thinking is not aimed simply at reaching a verbal agreement, more or less temporary, as to how we might speak of God, but also at mutually transforming the sensibility, the comportment towards the world, that we live out in our bodily life (a life that is itself intrinsically social and interactive). The way in which we attend to and deploy the

---

[2] Nor, to be fair, is it the only way actually practised by critics.

dimension of the figural in what we say will be vital in furthering this larger aim and will go a long way towards determining the kind of outcome we look for and achieve.

From the verbal to the visual

But it doesn't stop there, for just as the realm of human communication is larger than that of language, so too the realm of the image is larger than that of the figural dimension of language. We use images in ways that extend far beyond the perspectives on the world opened up by language. We are not just speaking animals, we are also seeing animals, and we communicate with each other no less by the sharing of visions than in our words.

This partly reiterates the point already made concerning body-language, since body-language itself communicates chiefly by means of sight. As I see your face redden, your mouth tighten and your brows begin to knot together I know that you are getting angry with me, even before you say anything. When I see you sitting alone, deflated, fallen in upon yourself and slumped in your chair, I know that something pretty major is up with you. Theatre and cinema (and, as we have seen, religious art) make very good use of this visual quality of body language. I see a group of characters on stage or screen and I see at once who is the strong one, who is the outsider, who is the villain of the piece. The tone of voice, the expression of the eyes or the posture of a speaker can serve to corroborate his speech, or it can make me, as spectator, realize his insincerity.[3]

---

[3] And, of course, as drama gets more sophisticated it is able to intimate that all is not what it seems, and that the man whom I (and the other *dramatis personae*) took to be sincere is, in fact, a consummate deceiver. The possibilities are endless – but the language of the body continues to provide a communicative resource no less important than the written text of the play. No less – yet important in a different way and, as we know, *how* a play is performed can involve radical reconceptions of familiar roles. Tone of voice, movement, position and gesture can be used to confirm or to qualify the villainy of a Shylock or a Richard III, to damn or to redeem the pride of Malvolio, to celebrate the love of Romeo and Juliet or to debunk it.

But vision does not just exist in the service of speech, it also reaches into regions of experience and understanding that language never penetrates – and if dramatic art is where we might best look to see how body-language can inform and extend spoken utterance, it is naturally the visual arts that lead us to the further reaches of the purely visual.[4]

The point may seem simple, but it is not uncontroversial. As with body language, there are ways of approaching and understanding art that turn it into a kind of language rather than accepting it as a relatively autonomous domain of human experience and practice. Moreover, some types of art have themselves gone along with this. Allegory has sometimes seemed to reduce images into pictograms, and even colour, often regarded as the most purely non-verbal element in art, has been codified and turned into something like a sign-language. Nor is the autonomy of art as self-evident as it may seem to us in the wake of Romanticism and Modernism. Without speculating as to the earliest origins and history of art we can see that art in the Middle Ages had a very different relation to the text of the Bible from that which developed after the Renaissance. The image only gradually loosens itself from the text, and whilst the genius of the manuscript illustrator could do astonishing things within the prescriptive constraints of the enframing text, the possibilities for artistic freedom opened up by the early Renaissance really were something else again. For many critics and historians what was then inaugurated was a process leading towards the complete emancipation of art from any outside influences, something complete in the era of high Modernism and the reduction of painting to the 'pure' visuality of the two-dimensional picture

---

[4] This is not, of course, to say that the visual arts have exclusive rights in this matter. Just as body-language is not the preserve of actors, so too vision is not the sole property of artists. If Ruskin was right, there is already a communicative dynamic in the very way in which the visible world reveals itself to the eye: the outlines of a landscape, the forms of clouds and vegetation and the colours and tones of light are the primary basis on which art itself first becomes possible.

plane. On this view of things, art as the opening up and exploration of pure visuality is far from naive, but is the end-result of a long and tangled history in which the struggles between word and image, convention and freedom have been repeatedly re-enacted in ever-new contexts and under ever-changing conditions. Pure vision is not where art begins but where it arrives.

Nevertheless, it is worth considering whether even the simplest picture, and even the picture designed to serve as a 'mere' illustration of a verbal text, doesn't in fact achieve its distinctive effect by disclosing a way of perceiving and a way of communicating that is different from the ways of language. And if this is true of an everyday illustration, how much more is it true of works that are thoroughly painterly. What we can say about painting (or drawing or sculpture) never exhausts what there is to see in it. The most complete historical, critical and descriptive account of a work by Rembrandt or Manet or de Kooning will inevitably fall short of the work itself, and we will always need to return to the work to renew our visual sense of what it means to us. This is not an easy process. The critical culture of our time, a culture propagated through newspapers, radio and television and popular art journals as well as through higher-level critical and philosophical writing, generates a climate of expectations and predisposes us to respond in particular ways to particular works. I will look at a painting one way if I believe it to be by Rembrandt, in another way if it is merely 'attributed' to Rembrandt, in another way again if it is from the 'school of' Rembrandt and in yet another way if it is by just another unknown Dutch seventeenth-century painter. Instead of being led by my eye, I am led by the accompanying caption. I don't 'see' what I actually see, but what I think I see or what I believe I ought to see. Even when the critical expectation I bring to a work or refine in the light of my response to the work is not of this superficial and trivializing kind, the painting still opens a view beyond that which can be rehearsed in words, and to understand the meaning of the critical discourse itself I must be prepared to let go of my verbal apparatus and give myself over to just looking.

'Pure Romanticism!' some may say, but this is to presume that 'just looking' is itself a mindless, contentless act. As with body language, the kind of communication that occurs in and through painting is analogous to verbal language, and once more that means dissimilarity as well as similarity. Here perhaps the dissimilarity is greater and the similarity less, but the realm of the image, *precisely in its difference from that of language*, is not thereby thoughtless. Perhaps the keenest art critics of all are not the reviewers and aestheticists, but those artists (Manet and Picasso are outstanding examples in the modern era) whose work is itself a critical response to and thereby a radical transformation of the traditions of art. Just as we previously spoke about the relationship between the *novum* of religious experience requiring interpretation in the light of tradition, so too in art new ways of seeing and painting provoke an often dramatic revisiting of the remote or recent past at the same time as they open a path towards the future.

The vision of the artist is not the simple reflex of aimless looking at the world but the fruit of a complex and transformative set of reactions to the realm of the visible, including what others have wrought in this realm. Pure seeing is not white light, but an intelligent, passionate and critical response to the visual revelations of art and nature. Discipline and discernment are no less relevant here than in the case of language, although it is a different kind of discipline and a different kind of discernment. It is not simply a lower or more primitive stage of what achieves a more adequate form in language.

The difference, however, is not such as to preclude our speaking of 'dialogue' in relation to visual communication in art, or in the wider realm of the visual that art consciously – artfully! – represents. In this way, we can begin to see how dialogue cannot be limited to language, as conventionally understood. Art is not, however, the only way of expanding our sense for what is involved in thorough-going dialogism. We might develop similar thoughts in relation to music and the role of sound and rhythm in shaping our common life-world. We might even learn from therapies involving smell and touch to include these more 'irrational' senses and their corresponding objects in the overall construction of human meaning. I shall not, however, pursue these reflections any further here, partly because I am not competent to do so, and partly because the direction in which I would wish to develop them should by now be clear. In each case we would be seeking to widen the range of forms and processes of communication considered relevant to thinking about God far beyond those usually regarded as definitive by philosophy and theology. Whatever we think about God is incomplete until we have allowed our thinking so to immerse itself in the stream of more-than-linguistic meaning that is saturated and moulded by the vital currents flowing there. If this statement can be reproached with trading the 'knowledge' once pursued by theology for the 'passion' of a more visceral, more incarnational way of thinking about God, I should emphasize that, as conceived here, 'passion' is neither thoughtless nor directionless. It is itself a kind of lived interpretation, the shaper, bearer and revealer of meanings and intentions.

Thinking about God will, it should be added, find more than enough in this extension of the structures of meaning to compensate for the loss of the metaphysical high ground of classical ontology. At the same time, it is important to emphasize that what is being proposed here is not a naturalistic reduction of theology. In thus expanding the scope of thinking about God to take in the full compass of incarnate life, I am not suggesting that biology or what is normally regarded as the subconscious provide a repository of ready-made meanings we can simply tap. Metaphysical objectivity is not being traded in for the sake of naturalistic objectivity, and language is not being reduced to the status of a mere epiphenomenon of animal behaviour. If anything, the opposite is the case. Precisely because the dimensions of pre- and extra-linguistic meaning are being claimed as the stuff of dialogue, they are being reclaimed from the dominion of supposedly unconscious forces and treated as areas for which we are answerable. Far from dissolving the ideal of human freedom into a multiplicity of sub-personal processes, what is being recommended here points to a widening and deepening of the scope of freedom and of our responsibility towards ourselves and others.

Towards the ethical

One final set of considerations should serve to clarify the issue. What is being proposed here is not just a matter of getting in touch with our bodies or our subconscious, though these are in their own way perfectly legitimate goals. They are not merely desirable for their own sake, however, nor yet for the sake of maximally expanding my possibilities of self-awareness. Dialogical thinking is not reducible to self-cultivation or self-discovery, but is orientated from the ground up by the reciprocity of self and other. As a rider to this it might be added that, despite the importance of poetry and art as means of sensitizing ourselves to what is beyond words, what is being pursued here is not a simple aestheticizing of theology, as if a concern for literature or visual art could save theology from its spiral of decline. To widen the scope of theology in this way, like the enlargement of self-awareness, is an admirable thing in itself, but unless it is part of a more radical reorientation of the whole task of thinking about God, it will provide only temporary relief. A little bit more colour, a little bit more variety, a little bit more cultural credibility – these things are in themselves mere palliatives. They might make for attractive degree courses and keep the sap of public interest rising, but they should not be allowed to excuse the deferral of facing up to the underlying issues.

To recall the fact that dialogical thinking accepts without reserve its conditioning by the total interdependence of self and other at every level of experience, understanding and action, is in effect to say that the fundamental nature of such thinking is, in a broad sense, moral or ethical. In allowing our thinking to be shaped by the mutual implication of self and other we commit ourselves to placing principles such as responsibility, answerability and trust at the very centre of our intellectual project. Dialogism is not – as has been emphasized at a number of points – merely an attempt to salvage the subjective sense of individual self-awareness from the irresistible advance of the scientific and technological quantification and manipulation of life, since it is a fundamental premiss of the dialogical approach that my thinking can never hope to shed its obligation to the other. Responding to the provocation or inspiration of the other, dialogism is not a way of escaping the debt of intelligibility I owe to that other without whom my own thinking would have remained unformed, inchoate, and without direction.

This is, of course, not enough to justify calling such thinking moral or ethical in the normal sense, and it should be acknowledged that by describing it in this way I am implicitly calling for an enlargement of what we mean by 'the ethical' analogous to the enlargement of critical thought invoked by appealing to the realms of the pre- and extra-linguistic. Such an enlargement is, however, perfectly intelligible in terms of ethics itself. For many moral philosophers and religious moralists have drawn attention to the need not to limit the scope of our mutual responsibilities to the consideration of issues of right and wrong action, narrowly conceived. At an everyday level, we are probably all familiar with the case of people who do the right thing in such a way as to depress or dishearten all around them. Although Saint Paul counsels us to do good to our enemies in order that we may heap coals of fire on their heads, we are uncomfortable with the moral policy implied in his advice. Surely the aim of good conduct is to liberate the world of interpersonal relationships from cycles of bitterness and hatred, and not simply to redeem ourselves at the expense of others. Wasn't Kierkegaard on better ground when he argued that it would be wrong to allow ourselves to become martyrs for the truth if we thereby made others guilty of our deaths? Or, to put the matter at its simplest: it's not what you do, it's the way that you do it. If we only have regard to the rightness of a particular course of action as judged by the standard of some external moral law or by the extent to which it may satisfy our individual desire for a clean conscience, then we are likely to find ourselves being condemned as pharisaical (in the popular sense of the term). The doctor who tells me I have terminal cancer may thereby fulfil his duty towards me, but if he does not take care to do so in an appropriate tone of voice and in language I can understand, and if he is not prepared to give me time to let the news sink in or to listen to my questions and anxieties, then I may well end up thinking him a brute (even though I may acknowledge that the abruptness of his manner is his way of dealing with what must, for him too, be a distressing situation). It is not enough to do the right thing. We have to do it in such a way that it is able to be received as such by others. Courtesy, Charles Williams said somewhere, is the first law of the Kingdom of Heaven. To practise this, however, we need precisely to have the most inclusive awareness of what belongs to the integrity of personality, both in ourselves and in others. Awareness, sensitivity, tact, 'the bedside manner' or approachability are not of themselves moral virtues, but without the kind of attentive openness to others suggested by such terms, 'morality' is likely to fall far short of its goal of increasing human good.

I am not blind to the fact that what has just been said may sound like a recipe for confusing the nice and the good, for aestheticizing morality or for reducing the ethical into mere social acceptability. If we are so concerned to attune our morality to the sensitivities of our neighbours, won't we end up by succumbing to the fate that, in the popular mind, has befallen the clergy of the Church of England; that is, our anxiety not to offend will displace our commitment to the challenge and discipline of prophetic morality. ('More tea, vicar?' 'But I'd come to talk to you about your infidelity to your husband . . . your investments in arms production . . .') Won't the truly moral person be one who is willing and able to stand against the crowd, alone against the world, as and when need arises? Offence may not be intended, but if doing the right thing is offensive, then surely it is better to lose the love and sympathy of the world than to damage the moral integrity of our own souls? Isn't there a point at which we have to stop talking and act? Dialogue may help us to contain human conflicts, but it cannot resolve them.

The only way to do that is through committed action. One doesn't talk to Nazis.

Several comments may be made in reply to this.

In the first place, whilst the main thrust of the objection is doubtless true, I suspect that in modern Western culture, nourished on several generations' worth of propaganda on behalf of the prophetic rebel, standing alone against a hostile and misunderstanding world in order to expose the hypocrisies of bourgeois convention that stand in the way of a free and authentic life,[5] the self-gratification of assuming such a prestigious role often blinds us to the issue as to whether it is appropriate or not. The transgression of social taboos and moral boundaries has become an end in itself in large areas of our contemporary culture, and many of us are all too determined to be rebels, with or without a cause. In terms of the age and climate in which we live, then, I suspect (and this is, of course, no more than a provisional, personal view) that we need to take more rather than less seriously the responsibility of considering the impact of our actions upon others.

That is as may be, and I certainly do not wish to deny that there are many silent sufferers who really do need the therapy of radical autonomy, who need to learn how to stand up for themselves and to break loose from constricting conventions and smothering domestic or social conditions. Certainly, if anything is obvious in the moral sphere it is that we should not simply overlook or indulge some heinous crime for the sake of a quiet life. Whilst we cannot expect everyone in a totalitarian state to rise to the heights of public defiance and heroic martyrdom, we will be disappointed in the moral capacities of our fellow human beings (or in our own moral capacities if we are in that situation) if no one stands up to be counted. In the actual exercise of morality, we will all, doubtless, find ourselves making many compromises. Not all moral goals are

---

[5] A role model that itself draws on religious archetypes of biblical prophecy, of Jesus's public ministry and of Luther's defiant 'Here I am, I can do no other!'

immediately achievable, and the very fact that we are continually having to choose between different goals, moving them up and down our agenda according to how we judge their relative importance, imposes the practical necessity of some compromise: I accept that I have to defer the pursuit of policy *a* in order to give myself time to pursue policy *b*. Furthermore, in pursuing *a* I encounter opposition of such a kind (whether it is the opposition of others or the realization of some weakness in myself) that I am forced to accept that I can only implement my long-term aim gradually or partially. 'I ought' may entail 'I can try', but it does not mean that I can, out of my own resources, deliver the sought-for result.

Such an acceptance of the necessity of tactical compromise is not, however, the same as allowing my very choice of action to be shaped by the spirit of responsiveness and answerability, and it is the latter which would seem more radically to undermine the very possibility of moral heroism. Given that it is probably easier to pose as a moral hero than to be one, surely it is still the case that self-choice, self-determination, self-direction must lie at the root of an action that is to have any good claim to be called moral. If every action I undertake is dialogically-determined, chosen and ordered according to my perception of the needs and sensibilities of others, how is it still moral?

The challenge posed by this question is serious. In reply I should like to venture three points.

The first point is that by enlarging our sense of what is involved in a genuinely personal interaction into the realm of what might be called the affective life we become able to see that much more is involved in ethical conduct than we often imagine. Morality does not itself exhaust the ways in which I can behave badly towards my neighbour, and the pursuit of perfect goodness must surely seek to identify and correct these other, less easily definable but no less affecting, ways. Now to reduce it to a matter of mere manners would be to trivialize this point. Sometimes it will probably be the case that I have to offend against the minor conventions and pleasantries of social exchange if I am to redress deep wrongs or promote important good. Sometimes I may need to spoil a friendship or outrage my colleagues by speaking an uncomfortable truth. But apart from the point, already made, that such occasions are likely to arise less often than we care to think and should not of themselves set the standard for our everyday moral comportment, my judgment of such issues will be the more convincing, the greater my conception of the heights and depths of personal life that lie beyond the appearances of public discourse. Naturally I should be wary of arrogating to myself an infallible intuition in such matters; precisely because we are moving beyond words into areas that involve assessing passions and affections for which there is no linguistic expression that does not require careful and considerate interpretation, any judgment we make will be in the spirit of fear and trembling, and we will do well to remain conscious of our own fallibility. Perhaps the 'brutal' doctor is right, perhaps it is better for the patient to undergo the short, sharp shock of a death sentence that does not permit of any ambiguity or uncertainty; perhaps it is only this approach that clears the way for the process of deep and genuine acceptance of the situation to begin. Perhaps. How we decide such issues is itself a matter that necessarily involves the opening up of our affective sensibilities. Certainly I will view the brusque doctor somewhat differently if I come to believe that his manner is not thoughtless but is intended to serve the good of his patients. Nonetheless, his good intentions are no guarantee that his way of behaving is the right one. To move the discussion from the level of simple right and wrong to that of sensibility is not to shut down the requirement of dialogue, but to extend it. It is to acknowledge that as moral agents we are accountable for more, far more, than we generally care to think. Such an acknowledgment should not unnerve us. We must still act, but the greater our awareness of all that is involved in the action, the more probable it is that the action itself will be appropriate and effective.

My second point is that to be influenced in our choice of moral ends and means by our perception of the personal integrity of those others with whom we have to do is not simply to become passive in relation to them. On the contrary, the dialogically-determined quest for what is authentically personal is necessarily active. The dialogist is no 'respecter of persons' precisely because that towards which dialogical thinking is directed is the personal. It will in every case remain open to question whether the actual life being lived in the world by an individual or a collectivity genuinely incarnates the values of personality – or whether it suppresses and conceals them.

My third point – and it is unashamedly not an original one – is that the ethical is not being pursued here for the sake of developing or demonstrating my own moral excellence. In relation to ethics the way of dialogue is, to put it at its simplest, the way of love, and love has an awkward relation to right and wrong. Love is able to forego rights and to overlook wrongs, 'to hide a multitude of sins'. From the standpoint of morality this will occasionally seem downright immoral, a conflict of views that is paradigmatically exemplified in the Gospel accounts of the confrontations between Jesus and his more legalistic contemporaries.[6] Perhaps it is a good principle to say that we shouldn't talk to Nazis – but does it follow that we shouldn't admit Sinn Fein to the conference table?

In saying that the thrust of my argument here is towards ethics and the realm of moral action, I am also implicitly saying that it points towards the political. For just as the dynamics of inter-personal action are only artificially limited to the plane of conventional moral categories and need to be extended into what I have been calling our affective sensibility, such action will also inevitably overflow the model of one-on-one personal interaction. Dialogical morality, like dialogical discourse, can never be simply a matter of I-and-Thou (although it cannot be less than that) but will necessarily involve the multiplicity of relationships in which each

---

[6] It is, of course, highly regrettable and a travesty of the truth to use these confrontations to define the difference between church and synagogue. Such an illegitimate extension of their meaning is itself a crime against the spirit of love.

I and each Thou have come to be what they are, and towards which each is responsible. But politics too must learn (as its best practitioners have long since learned) that the formulation and implementation of policy is not just a matter of addressing the conscious and stated needs and desires of citizens. Politics, like ethics, also involves assessing qualitative dimensions of human good, and only if it does so will it genuinely promote human flourishing. The principle of dialogue means, of course, that it cannot simply be left to the intuition and discernment of politicians to define such good. Willingly or not, they must repeatedly be summoned to the bar of dialogue and held accountable for the judgments they make and the actions they undertake on the basis of those judgments. Although politics must bring into play more than the calculations of prudential reason, it must not and cannot shed the discipline of dialogical responsibility. These remarks shed further light on my earlier comment that theology in the church has something of the character of rhetoric,[7] for rhetoric is fundamentally orientated towards the requirements of ethical and political action.

It is not my intention here to develop a dialogical politics any more than a dialogical ethics. In concluding with this brief discussion of these spheres, I am indicating that in speaking about a new kind of thinking about God that might yet emerge from under the rubble of metaphysics and dogma, I am not proposing a policy of mysticism or withdrawal from public life. Thinking about God is not undertaken for the sake of the thinker alone, for the alleviation of his solitude. The ethical and the political do not exhaust the task of dialogue, but dialogue can never dissociate itself from the responsibilities arising in those spheres. In choosing to discuss them at this point of the argument, where I have been seeking to point to those dimensions of dialogue that lie 'beyond words', I do not mean to suggest that moral or political decision-making occurs in some kind of wordless space. My intention is

---

[7] See Chapter 4 above.

rather to underline just how large is the scope and just how fearful is the task of seeking to be faithful to the obligation of dialogue in every dimension of life. I do not discharge this obligation by negotiating acceptable forms of words but by attending to and addressing deep human needs, and enhancing the all-round realization of human good.

We have, then, followed the path of dialogue from the sanctuary wherein we sought words for the mystery of personality, human and divine out into the profane world of culture and politics. We have done so, as was acknowledged at an early stage of our journey, at the distance appropriate to a purely theoretical approach, merely describing the conditions for a dialogical approach to thinking about God. Actually to carry out the work of such thinking would require more than the kind of brief outline this book has limited itself to being. Indeed, it would require more than the work of one individual. And more than the work of two. For dialogue does not mean simply an exchange of views between two parties, eyeball to eyeball in the conference chamber. In its fullest sense it is what the early Romantics called 'sym-philosophy', a term I should like loosely to translate as 'lovingly seeking wisdom together'. And when we have come from the personal to the political along this way of lovingly seeking wisdom together, it may happen that the way turns back upon itself and that in the midst of what seem to be the deserts of the secular a new path opens for us. Upon this path falls the light of the holy, transforming the everyday by the blessing of God amongst us. We cannot anticipate such moments, but we can wait upon them, and greet them when they are vouchsafed.